Literature-Based Reading Activities —

Second Edition

Hallie Kay Yopp
California State University, Fullerton

Ruth Helen Yopp
California State University, Fullerton

Allyn and Bacon

Boston   London   Toronto   Sydney   Tokyo   Singapore

Deb Marciano

Executive Editor: Virginia Lanigan
Editorial Assistant: Nihad Farooq
Executive Marketing Manager: Kathy Hunter
Production Administrator: Annette Joseph
Production Coordinator: Holly Crawford
Editorial-Production Service: Laura Cleveland/WordCrafters Editorial
      Services Inc.
Composition Buyer: Linda Cox
Manufacturing Buyer: Megan Cochran
Cover Administrator: Suzanne Harbison
Cover Designer: Jenny Burns

Library of Congress Cataloging-in-Publication Data

Yopp, Hallie Kay.
    Literature-based reading activities / Hallie Kay Yopp, Ruth Helen
Yopp.—2nd ed.
    p.   cm.
    Ruth Helen Yopp appears first on the earlier edition.
    Includes bibliographical references and index.
    ISBN 0-205-16387-4
    1. Reading (Elementary)   2. Literature—Study and teaching
(Elementary)   I. Yopp, Ruth Helen.   II. Title.
LB1573.Y67   1995
372.6'4044—dc20   95-37380
                                                              CIP

Printed in the United States of America
10 9 8 7 6 5 4 3 2 1   00 99 98 97 96 95

Credit: pp. 25–27 from *Where the Readers Are* (pp. 22–23) by C. F.
Reasoner, 1972, New York: Dell. Copyright 1972 by Delacorte Press, a
division of Bantam, Doubleday, Dell Publishing Group, Inc. Adapted by
permission.

To Peter, Erica, Billy, and Danny
and
their Grandpa Bill

Contents

Preface _____

This book arose from a need to compile a number of activities that may be used with a wide variety of literature selections in classroom settings. Too many teachers have spent too much money on ditto books for individual works of literature. Often these ditto books provide page after page of low-level, skills-based, one-correct-answer-only worksheets. They lack imagination and are contrary to the rationale for using literature in the classroom. In contrast, the activities in this book are open-ended, encourage critical thinking and discussion, and serve as springboards for writing. In addition, they are generic in nature; that is, they are not specific to a particular reading selection and are easily implemented with virtually any piece of literature.

As we worked with preservice and inservice kindergarten through eighth-grade teachers who were beginning to implement literature-based reading programs, we were encouraged to record these ideas in a book. The activities presented here come from a wide variety of sources, including professional conferences and workshops, journals, books, classroom teachers, and student teachers. All have been classroom tested and many have been the subject of research. We are grateful for all that we have learned from our colleagues, our students, and classroom teachers.

The organization of the second edition of this book remains the same as the first edition. Chapter One provides a rationale for using literature in the classroom and describes teachers' responsibilities when using literature. New to this chapter is a discussion of some of the issues related to implementing a literature-based reading program. The chapter also delineates the criteria we used in selecting activities to include in this book. For purposes of organization, activities have been identified as pre-, during-, or postreading activities to coincide with phases in the instructional cycle. However, many of the activities can be used at any or all phases of instruction. The activities are found in Chapters Two, Three, and Four, along with examples of their application at several grade levels. Each activity may be used at any grade level; indeed, we have used them with kindergarten through university students. Examples are provided from a variety of genre, including folktales, fantasy, realistic fiction, historical fiction, poetry, biography, and informational books. For many of the examples, samples of actual student responses are provided. These responses are not intended to reflect "good" answers, however. Many of these activities tap students' interests, attitudes, and experiences; therefore, responses will be as diverse as the students. The second edition offers five new activities: character webs, character journals, plot organizers, world wheels, and table talk. In addition, the reader will find that approximately half of the examples provided for the activities throughout the book are new.

Because one of the most exciting ways to extend the literature experience is for students to construct their own books, Chapter Five remains devoted to the construction of individual and classroom books. A few important final comments are offered in the Afterword, and lists of professional resources and winners of two of the most coveted awards for children's literature, the Newbery and the Caldecott, are included in appendices.

We hope the reader will find the activities presented here worthwhile and that they stimulate considerable thinking, writing, discussion, and enthusiasm for reading in the classroom.

We wish to acknowledge the following reviewers who provided helpful comments about the book: Ann Hall, Southwest Texas State University; Katharine G. Fralick, Plymouth State College; and Dale Sakrison, Bemidji State University.

We are grateful to the following people for their contributions to this book: Nancy Brewbaker, Paula Gray, and Alan Saldivar, Example 3.15; Doreen Fernandez, Janie Frigge, Kimberly Hennessy, and Thursa Williams, Example 4.3; and Jeanine Rossi, retelling picture book example. We thank Darrell Guillaume and Andrea Guillaume for providing several of the graphics in this edition. We also thank our husbands, Bert Slowik and Tom Edwards, for the encouragement and support they provide. Finally, we thank our parents, William B. Yopp and Phyllis Jean Yopp, whose influence will be felt throughout our lifetimes.

CHAPTER ONE

Using Literature in the Classroom

Literature in the Classroom

Research and Issues	Teacher Responsibilities	Rationale for Selection of Activities
■ Language development ■ Reading comprehension ■ Perceptions of reading act ■ Attitudes toward reading ■ Writing ability ■ Patterns of instruction ■ Reader stance	■ Read the selection ■ Identify themes ■ Plan pre-, during-, and postreading activities ■ Create an atmosphere of trust	■ Promote grand conversations ■ Develop background knowledge ■ Promote integration of the language arts ■ Promote higher-level thinking ■ Are appropriate for variety of grouping styles ■ Are useful with ESL students

The increase of interest in and use of literature in classrooms in the past several years has been characterized as a revolution (McGee, 1992). Indeed, one can rarely pick up an issue of a professional language arts journal, browse through a conference program, skim the pages of an educational publications catalog, or walk down the aisles of a teacher supply store without seeing titles related to the use of literature in the language arts program and across the curriculum. Teachers are encouraged to surround their students with rich, authentic, whole pieces of literature from the earliest grades and to place children's literature at the core of their reading programs. In classrooms across the nation, a new emphasis on promoting a love of reading is replacing an emphasis on skills.

Contributing to this shift was research cited in the report of the Commission on Reading (Anderson, Hiebert, Scott, & Wilkinson, 1985) that 70 percent of elementary students' reading instructional time is spent on independent workbook pages and skill sheets, and that these activities are unrelated to gains in reading achievement. At the same time, evidence was accumulating that reading literature aloud to students is imperative for building the background knowledge necessary for success in reading (Anderson et al., 1985), and that the amount of time children spend reading in school is associated with gains in reading achievement (Foertsch, 1992). Yet, according to the 1990 and 1992 National Assessment of Educational Progress (NAEP) reports, children do very little reading in school. Indeed, approximately one-half of the students in grades four, eight, and twelve assessed by the NAEP in both 1988 and 1990 reported reading ten or fewer pages each day for schoolwork across the curriculum (Foertsch, 1992; Langer, Applebee, Mullis, & Foertsch, 1990).

How are children to find the joy in reading if their classroom experiences are limited to worksheets? How can teachers encourage students to become lifelong readers if they rarely ask them to read? It is only through meaningful literary experiences that children develop an enthusiasm for reading. Few basal readers and skill sheets stimulate hearts and minds the way books do.

Huck, Hepler, and Hickman (1993) state that the intrinsic personal values of literature alone should be sufficient to give literature a place in the curriculum. In addition to the personal value of using literature, however, there is considerable evidence of its educational value. For example, the use of literature has been shown to facilitate language development in both younger and older children. Chomsky (1972) found a positive correlation between six- to ten-year-old students' exposure to stories and their performance on several measures of linguistic development. She recommended that an effort be made "towards providing more and richer language exposure, rather than limiting the child with restrictive and carefully programmed materials" (p. 33). Nagy, Herman, and Anderson (1985) examined eighth-grade students' vocabulary acquisition after reading expository and narrative text and concluded that "a most effective way to produce large-scale vocabulary growth is through an activity that is all too often interrupted in the process of reading instruction: Reading" (p. 252). Krashen (1989) also has argued that reading is the best way to teach vocabulary.

Exposure to literature also has been demonstrated to result in reading comprehension gains. Cohen (1968) compared the reading achievement of second-grade children who received systematic daily exposure to literature at school to that of children who only occasionally heard stories at school. She found that the former group significantly outperformed the latter on reading comprehension measures at the end of the school year. Similar results were reported by Feitelson, Kita, and Goldstein (1986) and DeFord (1981), the latter of whom suggested that literature offers more to comprehend than controlled-vocabulary reading materials, and thus comprehension becomes a natural part of the process. Morrow, O'Connor, and Smith (1990) compared the effects of a storybook reading program with a traditional reading readiness program that emphasized letter recognition and letter-sound correspondence on the literacy development of "at-risk" kindergarteners. Those children who engaged in literature experiences significantly outperformed their peers in the traditional readiness program on measures of comprehension and attempted readings of favorite stories taken at the end of the year.

In addition, there is evidence that students' perceptions of and attitudes toward reading are influenced by literature-based reading programs. An exploratory study conducted by Hagerty, Hiebert, and Owens (1989) not only contributed further evidence of superior comprehension performance by students (in this case, second, fourth and sixth graders) involved in a literature-based reading instructional program when compared to children participating in a skills-based reading curriculum, but also revealed that students in literature-based classrooms changed their perceptions of reading and writing over the course of the year in the program. Their views of these processes shifted from a skills-based view to a meaning-based view. Hagerty et al. argued that students' perceptions of the reading and writing processes are determined by the instruction they receive and that these perceptions may impact students' facility in reading and writing.

A study by Eldredge and Butterfield (1986) provided evidence for the intuitively appealing notion that the use of literature results in significantly more positive attitudes toward reading in young children than the use of basal readers, in addition to considerable achievement effects. Larrick (1987) and Tunnell and Jacobs (1989) also documented the marked improvement in attitudes toward reading when students were involved in a literature-based reading program.

Because literature serves as a model of effective language, its use also influences students' writing ability. Indeed, research reveals that children's writing styles reflect the written language to which they are exposed. For example, Eckhoff (1983) found that children using text that closely matches the style and complexity of literary prose wrote more elaborate sentences by including subordinate clauses, infinitive phrases, and participial phrases, and that they used more complex verb forms than children who read simplified text such as that found in many traditional basal readers. Children in the latter group tended to imitate the simple, repetitive language they encountered in those texts in their own writing. Other research has demonstrated that children in literature-based reading programs incorporate a wider variety of literary forms, such as poems, songs, informational text, stories, and newspaper reports, into their written repertoires than children in skills-based reading programs (DeFord, 1981, 1984).

Morrow (1992) investigated the effects of a combination of literature-based instruction with traditional basal reader instruction on the literacy achievement, use of literature, and attitudes toward reading of children from diverse backgrounds. When compared to students who received only basal reader instruction, the students receiving literature-based instruction performed better on oral and written comprehension tasks, story development tasks, language complexity and vocabulary tasks, and attitude measures. No difference was found between the groups on a standardized reading test.

Few would argue with the value of using literature in reading programs. What is currently under discussion among teachers and researchers is how to use literature. Based on observations of elementary classrooms, Zarrillo (1989) identified three patterns of literature use: the core book, characterized by all students reading or listening to the same book and then participating in assignments related to the book; the literature unit, characterized by a balance between common activities and student-selected activities; and individualized reading with self-selection and self-pacing, characterized by student choice of books and activities and regular teacher-student conferences.

Hiebert and Colt (1989) also identified patterns of literature-based reading instruction, and they argued that diverse patterns should be combined to form a comprehensive literature-based reading program. Using the two dimensions of literature selection and instructional format, Hiebert and Colt describe the following three patterns of literature-based reading instruction: teacher-selected literature in teacher-led groups, teacher- and student-selected literature in teacher- and student-led small groups, and student-selected literature read independently. Each of these patterns of instruction contributes to and is necessary for effective literacy instruction, for, as Hiebert and Colt state, "[w]hen teachers focus only on independent reading of student-selected material, they fail to consider the guidance that students require for becoming expert readers" (p. 19) and "children will not gain the . . . alternative points of view that are necessary to be proficient readers" (p. 18). On the other hand, "[a] focus on teacher-led instruction fails to develop the independent reading strategies that underlie lifelong reading" (p. 19).

Another issue that has received attention in recent years is how readers interact with literature. Rosenblatt (1991) believes that students need to develop the ability to read efferently and aesthetically; that is, to both gather information from the text and experience the text. The stance the students take when reading should depend on their purposes for reading and the situation. Teachers, of course, can and do influence students' transactions with text. If teachers quiz students after they read or listen to a selection, teachers are promoting an efferent stance; students learn that they read in order to retain information that might be asked for later by the teacher. However, if teachers encourage enjoyment of the reading experience and encourage personal responses to the reading; if they ask students to recapture the lived-through experience of the reading through drawing, dancing, talking, writing, or role playing, they are promoting an aesthetic stance on the part of the students. According to Rosenblatt and others (Ruddell, 1992; Zarrillo, 1991), students must develop the ability to adopt a stance along the efferent-aesthetic continuum that is most appropriate at a given time. Unfortunately, too often teachers encourage only an efferent stance, and thus do not encourage the real enjoyment of reading that is the primary goal of a literature-based program. It is critical that teachers keep in mind the intent of the movement toward literature-based reading instruction and heed the warning of Goodman (1988) who cautioned against the "basalization" of literature by treating books simply as vehicles for practicing skills.

The purpose of this book is to assist teachers in providing meaningful instruction when using literature. We have seen too many publications intended for literature-based programs that offer low-level, skills-based, one-correct-answer-only activities and worksheets. Instead, we offer a variety of activities that are open-ended, encourage critical thinking and discussion, focus on ideas in text, and allow for personal responses to literature. First, we present a brief list of teacher responsibilities that are critical to the successful implementation of directed literature experiences. Then we identify questions and answers that guided our search for activities to include in this book.

TEACHER RESPONSIBILITIES

For those teachers who have asked, "What can I do to ensure a successful experience with a book?" we offer the following suggestions:

1. *Read the book.* Simple as it may seem, it is extremely important that, prior to engaging students in a directed literature experience, you read the entire book yourself. It is not possible to plan the course of instruction without becoming familiar with the book.

2. *Identify themes in the book.* Many books have multiple themes. *Island of the Blue Dolphins* by Scott O'Dell, for example, examines loneliness, traditions, and survival. You should select the themes that are most appropriate for your students, that can be integrated with other curricula areas, or that parallel other books the students have read.

3. *Plan activities for three stages of study: before, during, and after reading the book.* Prereading activities should spark students' curiosity and activate relevant background knowledge. During-reading activities should promote comprehension and call attention to effective uses of language. Postreading activities should extend students' thinking about ideas, events, or characters in the book and promote connections between the book and real life or between one book and another. These activities should relate to the themes of the book that have been identified for study.

4. *Establish an atmosphere of trust.* Students will honestly communicate their feelings, experiences, and ideas only if there is an atmosphere of trust in the classroom. You can promote trust by respecting all student attempts to share and by allowing for a variety of interpretations of the meaning of a selection as long as the reader can support his or her ideas on the basis of the language in the text. Disagreements among students will lead back to the book and result in a closer analysis of the author's words.

RATIONALE FOR SELECTION OF ACTIVITIES FOR THIS BOOK

The following questions guided our search for activities to include in this book.

1. *Will the activity promote grand conversations about books?* "Grand conversations" can be best described by contrasting them to the "gentle inquisitions" that take place in many classrooms (Bird, 1988; Edelsky, 1988). During grand conversations, students are encouraged to think, feel, and respond to ideas, issues, events, and characters in a book. They are invited to express their opinions, and their opinions are valued. Personal involvement with the ideas contained in the book is encouraged, and individual interpretations are permissible as long as they are supported with data from the text. Grand conversations are similar to the discussions that occur in adult book groups in that the focus is on topics that are meaningful to the participants, and everyone is encouraged to contribute.

During "gentle inquisitions," on the other hand, the tone of the classroom interaction is one of "checking up" on the students. The teacher asks questions, and the students answer them. Although it is appropriate to assess students' comprehension, studies have revealed that a great deal of reading instructional time is spent asking students questions for the purpose of assessing their comprehension (Durkin, 1979; Wendler, Samuels, & Moore, 1989), and that higher-level reasoning activities such as discussing and analyzing what has been read are not routinely emphasized for students (Langer et al., 1990). Allington (1994) agrees that children "need substantially less interrogation and substantially more opportunities to observe and engage in conversations about books, stories, and other texts they have read" (p. 23).

The activities provided in this book can be used to stimulate grand conversations. They provide teachers with a structure for encouraging students to express their ideas honestly and share their thoughts and experiences with their peers. Thus, they provide an alternative to the traditional question-and-answer discussion format that usually focuses on correctness, can discourage meaningful conversations, and often limits participation to the most verbal children in the class.

2. *Will the activity develop and/or activate background knowledge?* Recent research reveals that a reader's organized knowledge of the world provides the basis for his or her comprehension of ideas in texts. This organized knowledge is referred to as a reader's *schema*. Comprehension is said to occur only when a reader can mentally activate a schema that offers an adequate account of the objects, events, and relationships described in a text (Anderson, 1984). The following sentence offered by Bransford and McCarrell (1974) illustrates this phenomenon: *The notes were sour because the seam split.* The vocabulary is not difficult and the sentence is short, yet it probably makes little sense to you. However, if you have any knowledge of bagpipes and you read this sentence in the context of bagpipes, it is no longer incomprehensible. Your schema of bagpipes accounts for all the elements in the sentence: the split seam, the sour notes, and the cause-effect relationship between the two. Failure to activate, or call to mind, an appropriate schema results in poor comprehension. An effective teacher promotes comprehension in his or her students by providing experiences that encourage them to access relevant knowledge prior to encountering a text. If students do not have the relevant background knowledge, then an effective teacher will help the students acquire the appropriate knowledge.

Many of the activities described in this book, especially those recommended for use before reading, are ideal for activating and building background knowledge. They require students to think about experiences they have had or to articulate their opinions on topics about which they will subsequently read. Students with limited background knowledge on a particular topic will benefit from listening to the comments of peers.

3. *Will the activity provide opportunities for reading, writing, listening, and speaking?* In *Becoming a Nation of Readers*, Anderson et al. (1985) argued that reading must be seen as part of a child's general language development and not as a discrete skill isolated from listening, speaking, and writing. Listening, speaking, reading, and writing are interrelated and mutually supportive, and classroom experiences must reflect this. Literacy experts encourage teachers to help their students understand the connection among these language skills (DeFord, 1981; Heilman, Blair, & Rupley, 1990; Heller, 1991; Holdaway, 1979; Searfoss & Readence, 1989; Shanahan, 1988).

Each of the activities described in this book provides opportunities for the integration of the language arts. None of the activities is intended to be reproduced on ditto paper and independently completed by silent students. Rather, the activities should serve as vehicles for discussions and are designed to inspire students to articulate their ideas and listen and respond to the ideas of others. Writing should be a natural outgrowth of the speaking, listening, and reading experiences.

4. *Does the activity promote higher-level thinking?* Many teachers are familiar with Bloom's (1956) taxonomy of educational objectives, a hierarchical classification system identifying levels of cognitive processing or thinking. The levels of the taxonomy from lowest to highest are knowledge, comprehension, application, analysis, synthesis, and evaluation. The lower levels, knowledge and comprehension, involve the ability to recall information and to understand it. The higher levels— application, analysis, synthesis, and evaluation—involve the ability to apply information learned, classify, compare and contrast, explain ideas or concepts, create, and evaluate or judge. According to Bloom (1984), educational practices, including the selection of instructional materials and the teaching methods used, seldom rise above the knowledge level. Similar conclusions were reported in the 1990 NAEP document (Langer et al., 1990) which revealed that students appear to have great difficulty with tasks requiring them to explain or elaborate on what they read, and that activities that promote higher-level reasoning, such as discussing, analyzing, or writing about what has been read, are not emphasized routinely in U.S. classrooms.

The activities included in this book serve to facilitate higher-level thinking. They provide opportunities for active interchange among students and encourage students to think and write about ideas that have been or will be confronted in the reading selection. They require students to compare and contrast characters and books, diagram relationships, and support their opinions with examples from the text. Many of the activities encourage creativity.

5. *Can the activity be used with heterogeneous groups of students?* Few would argue with the statement that all students should have the opportunity to interact with good literature. Unfortunately, however, in their efforts to meet the needs of less-prepared or less-able readers, many teachers limit these students to short prose and to worksheets and activities addressing only low-level cognitive skills. Poor readers are typically isolated from their more able peers and have neither the opportunity to share in a literature experience nor the opportunity to participate in the grand conversations about books that other students enjoy. Indeed, children in low-ability groups have been shown to receive less instruction and qualitatively different instruction than children in high-ability groups (Allington, 1980, 1984, 1994; Anderson et al., 1985; Bracey, 1987; Walmsley & Walp, 1989; Wuthrick, 1990). Because of the problems inherent in ability grouping, many experts recommend that alternatives be explored (Anderson et al., 1985).

One alternative is whole-class instruction. This option may be frightening to teachers who have spent years organizing their reading instruction around high-, average-, and low-ability groups. Many teachers have expressed concerns about working with all students simultaneously. One of the advantages of the activities presented in this book is that they can be easily and successfully implemented with all students in whole-classroom settings. Students of all ability levels can participate in the activities. Some students may respond at a higher level than others, but each student can contribute and each can benefit from listening to the experiences and opinions of his peers.

A second alternative is the use of cooperative learning groups in which students work in small heterogeneous groups to accomplish a common goal (Kagan, 1986; Slavin, 1983). Students may work in groups to respond to virtually any of the activities presented in this volume. When group members talk and listen to one another, they are activating their background knowledge and building upon it as they share ideas and make contributions. When they participate in prereading, during-reading, or postreading activities together, they are being exposed to a variety of thinking strategies and learning from one another. Students should be given many opportunities to work in cooperative groups.

In addition to whole-class and cooperative learning groups, other formats for organizing students include individuals, dyads, small groups, large groups, and half-class groups. Possible bases for group assignment include interest, students' choice, prior knowledge, social factors, work habits, and random assignment (Flood, Lapp, Flood, & Nagel, 1992).

It is our hope that teachers will use a variety of grouping patterns in their classrooms and neither form static ability groups nor be rigid about providing all instruction in a whole-class setting. Indeed, many educational leaders are calling for "flexible" grouping wherein students are grouped for a specific purpose, and when the purpose is achieved the group is disbanded (California Department of Education, 1994; Vogt, 1994).

6. *Can students who are learning English as a second language benefit from these activities?* Reading instruction should be offered in the primary language of the students while they are learning English. Many times, however, this is not possible due to limited resources in terms of both personnel and materials. Teachers must be careful as they attempt to meet the needs of these children not to isolate them from their classmates during reading instruction or to provide them with only low-level worksheets that emphasize discrete skills. Experiences with literature need not be withheld until students are fluent in English. Instructional practices, however, should be guided by our knowledge of effective techniques for teaching second-language learners.

In selecting the literature activities for this book, we considered what is known about appropriate instruction for second-language learners. Several principles guided our selection (Cummins, 1989; Kagan, 1986; Scarcella, 1990; Spangenberg-Urbschat & Pritchard, 1994). First, second-language learners should be provided with opportunities to listen, speak, read, and write in meaningful contexts. The activities included here offer many opportunities for students to share ideas and experiences through discussions and writing. Because they are asked to express their own experiences related to book content, these discussions are interesting and personally meaningful. Further, the focus is on communication. Second, information should not be presented in a strictly verbal format; visual representations of content aid comprehension. Many of the activities described in the book offer visual or graphic representations of themes or content. Third, many minority children perform better in cooperative and collaborative settings that encourage interaction than in individualistic, competitive settings. The activities presented here can be successfully used by pairs, small groups, or large groups. Fourth, instruction should focus on higher-level cognitive skills rather than factual recall. All of the activities included in this book promote higher-level thinking in the classroom. Fifth, modeling is important, especially for individuals learning a new language. The activities provide the opportunity for children to explain their thinking; thus, students serve as models for one another. Sixth, second-language learners are supported when purposes are set for reading. These activities serve to establish purposes before the students read, while they read, or as they revisit the text after reading.

CONCLUSION

There is considerable support for a movement toward greater use of literature in the classroom. In infusing their classrooms with literature, teachers must keep in mind that one of the primary reasons for using literature is to instill in children a love of reading. Thus, they must be extremely careful when making instructional decisions. Activities that reduce literature to a work to be fragmented and dissected and that do not deal with the essence or the meaning of the work violate the very core of a literature-based program. Indeed, such practices probably are more destructive than the complete omission of literature in a reading program. The activities in the next four chapters are in keeping with the spirit of the literature-based movement.

REFERENCES

Allington, R. (1980). Teacher interruption behaviors during primary-grade oral reading. *Journal of Educational Psychology, 72,* 371–377.

Allington, R. (1984). Content coverage and contextual reading in reading groups. *Journal of Reading Behavior, 16,* 85–96.

Allington, R. (1994). The schools we have. The schools we need. *The Reading Teacher, 48,* 14–29.

Anderson, R. (1984). Role of the reader's schema in comprehension, learning, and memory. In R. Anderson, J. Osborn, and R. Tierney, (Eds.), *Learning to read in American schools: Basal readers and content texts.* Hillsdale, NJ: Erlbaum.

Anderson, R., Hiebert, E., Scott, J., & Wilkinson, I. (1985). *Becoming a nation of readers: The report of the Commission on Reading.* Washington, DC: The National Institute of Education, U.S. Department of Education.

Bird, L. (1988). Reading comprehension redefined through literature study: Creating worlds from the printed page. *The California Reader, 21,* 9–14.

Bloom, B. (1956). *Taxonomy of educational objectives: Handbook I, cognitive domain.* New York: David McKay.

Bloom, B. (1984). The search for methods of group instruction as effective as one-to-one tutoring. *Educational Leadership, 41*(8), 4–17.

Bracey, G. (1987). The social impact of ability grouping. *Phi Delta Kappan, 68,* 701–702.

Bransford, J. D. & McCarrell, N. S. (1974). A sketch of a cognitive approach to comprehension. In W. B. Weimer & D. S. Palermo (Eds.), *Cognition and the symbolic processes.* Hillsdale, NJ: Erlbaum.

California Department of Education. (1994). *The framework in focus.* Sacramento: Author.

Chomsky, C. (1972). Stages in language development and reading exposure. *Harvard Educational Review, 42,* 1–33.

Cohen, D. (1968). The effect of literature on vocabulary and reading achievement. *Elementary English, 45,* 209–213, 217.

Cummins, J. (1989). *Empowering minority students.* Sacramento: California Association for Bilingual Education.

DeFord, D. (1981). Literacy: Reading, writing, and other essentials. *Language Arts, 58,* 652–658.

DeFord, D. (1984). Classroom contexts for literacy learning. In T. Raphael (Ed.), *The contexts of school-based literacy* (pp. 163–180). New York: Random House.

Durkin, D. (1979). What classroom observations reveal about reading comprehension instruction. *Reading Research Quarterly, 14,* 481–533.

Eckhoff, B. (1983). How reading affects children's writing. *Language Arts, 60,* 607–616.

Edelsky, C. (1988). Living in the author's world: Analyzing the author's craft. *The California Reader, 21,* 9–14.

Eldredge, J. & Butterfield, D. (1986). Alternatives to traditional reading instruction. *The Reading Teacher, 40,* 32–37.

Feitelson, D., Kita, B., & Goldstein, Z. (1986). Effects of listening to series stories on first graders' comprehension and use of language. *Research in the Teaching of English, 20,* 339–355.

Flood, J., Lapp, D., Flood, S., & Nagel, G. (1992). Am I allowed to group?: Using flexible patterns for effective instruction. *The Reading Teacher, 45,* 608–616.

Foertsch, M. (1992). *Reading in and out of school. Factors influencing the literacy achievement of American students in grades 4, 8, and 12, in 1988 and 1990.* Washington, DC: Office of Educational Research and Improvement, U.S. Department of Education.

Goodman, K. (1988). Look what they've done to Judy Blume!: The basalization of children's literature. *The New Advocate, 1,* 29–41.

Hagerty, P., Hiebert, E., & Owens, M. (1989). Students' comprehension, writing, and perceptions in two approaches to literacy instruction. In S. McCormick and J. Zutell (Eds.), *Cognitive and social perspectives for literacy research and instruction* (pp. 453–459). Chicago: National Reading Conference.

Heilman, A., Blair, T., & Rupley, W. (1990). *Principles and practices of teaching reading.* Columbus, OH: Merrill.

Heller, M. (1991). *Reading-writing connections: From theory to practice.* New York: Longman.

Hiebert, E., & Colt, J. (1989). Patterns of literature-based reading instruction. *The Reading Teacher, 43,* 14–20.

Holdaway, D. (1979). *The foundations of literacy.* Exeter, NH: Heinemann.

Huck, C., Hepler, S., & Hickman, J. (1993). *Children's literature in the elementary school* (5th ed.). Fort Worth: Harcourt Brace College Publishers.

Kagan, S. (1986). Cooperative learning and sociocultural factors in schooling. In *Beyond language: Social and cultural factors in schooling language minority students* (pp. 231–298). Los Angeles: Evaluation, Dissemination and Assessment Center, California State University.

Krashen, S. (1989). We acquire vocabulary and spelling by reading: Additional evidence for the input hypothesis. *The Modern Language Journal, 73*, 440–464.

Langer, J., Applebee, A., Mullis, I., & Foertsch, M. (1990). *Learning to read in our nation's schools: Instruction and achievement in 1988 at grades 4, 8, and 12. National Assessment of Educational Progress.* Princeton, NJ: Educational Testing Service.

Larrick, N. (1987). Illiteracy starts too soon. *Phi Delta Kappan, 69*, 184–189.

McGee, L. (1992). Focus on research: Exploring the literature-based reading revolution. *Language Arts, 69*, 529–537.

Morrow, L. M. (1992). The impact of a literature-based program on literacy achievement, use of literature, and attitudes of children from minority backgrounds. *Reading Research Quarterly, 27*, 250–275.

Morrow, L. M., O'Connor, E., and Smith, J. (1990). Effects of a story reading program on the literacy development of at risk kindergarten children. *Journal of Reading Behavior, 22*, 255–275.

Nagy, W., Herman, P., & Anderson, R. (1985). Learning words from context. *Reading Research Quarterly, 20*, 233–253.

O'Dell, S. (1960). *Island of the blue dolphins.* New York: Dell.

Rosenblatt, L. (1991). Literature—S.O.S.! *Language Arts, 68*, 444–448.

Ruddell, R. (1992). A whole language and literature perspective: Creating a meaning-making instructional environment. *Language Arts, 69*, 612–620.

Scarcella, R., (1990). *Teaching language minority students in the multicultural classroom.* Englewood Cliffs, NJ: Prentice Hall.

Searfoss, L. & Readence, J. (1989). *Helping children learn to read.* Englewood Cliffs, NJ: Prentice Hall.

Shanahan, T. (1988). The reading-writing relationship: Seven instructional principles. *The Reading Teacher, 41*, 756–761.

Slavin, R. (1983). *Cooperative learning.* New York: Longman.

Spangenberg-Urbschat, K., & Pritchard, R. (1994). *Kids come in all languages: Reading instruction for ESL students.* Newark, DE: International Reading Association.

Tunnell, M. & Jacobs, J. (1989). Using "real" books: Research findings on literature based reading instruction. *The Reading Teacher, 42*, 470–477.

Vogt, M. (1994). *Level the reading playing field with jumpstarting!* Presentation at the 28th annual conference of the California Reading

Association, Long Beach, CA, Nov. 3–5, 1994.

Walmsley, S., & Walp, T. (1989). *Teaching literature in elementary school.* Albany: Center for the Learning and Teaching of Literature, University at Albany, State University of New York.

Wendler, D., Samuels, S. J., & Moore, V. (1989). The comprehension instruction of award-winning teachers, teachers with master's degrees, and other teachers. *Reading Research Quarterly, 24,* 382–401.

Wuthrick, M. (1990). Blue jays win! Crows go down in defeat! *Phi Delta Kappan, 71,* 553–556.

Zarrillo, J. (1989). Teachers' interpretations of literature-based reading. *The Reading Teacher, 43,* 22–28.

Zarrillo, J. (1991). Theory becomes practice: Aesthetic teaching with literature. *The New Advocate, 4,* 221–234.

C H A P T E R   T W O

Prereading Activities _____

Prereading

Purposes	Activities
■ To build background knowledge	■ Anticipation guides
■ To activate background knowledge	■ Opinionnaires/ questionnaires
■ To elicit feelings	■ Contrast charts
■ To enhance identification with characters	■ Semantic maps
■ To set purposes for reading	■ KWL charts
■ To arouse curiosity	
■ To motivate	

The importance of engaging students in prereading activities cannot be overemphasized. It is through activities conducted prior to reading a selection that the teacher can build and activate students' background knowledge on topics or concepts contained in the book. As discussed in Chapter One, activation of relevant knowledge is fundamental to comprehension. Because children may not spontaneously integrate what they read with what they know, special attention should be paid to preparation for reading. If appropriate background knowledge cannot be assumed, knowledge-building activities should be provided.

In addition to building or activating background knowledge, prereading activities can provide a forum to elicit from students their feelings and reactions to ideas and issues contained in a reading selection before confronting those issues in the text. Such activities allow students to examine their own beliefs, enhance understanding and appreciation of events in the book or decisions made by characters, and encourage aesthetic responses to literature. Further, because they have thought about issues with which characters are confronted, students will identify more intensely with characters during reading. Prereading activities serve to set purposes for reading, arouse students' curiosity, and motivate them to read.

In this chapter, we describe five activities that may be used prior to reading a book, a chapter, or a passage. The first activity, the *anticipation guide*, prompts students to think about and take a stand on issues or concepts that they will later encounter. *Opinionnaires/questionnaires* are useful for tapping students' knowledge and previous related experiences as well as their beliefs and opinions on a subject. *Contrast charts* are ideal for helping students identify and articulate exemplars in opposing concepts. *Semantic maps*, graphic depictions of categorical information, serve to build and activate background knowledge. *KWL charts* provide a simple format for students to identify what they know about a topic and what questions they have about the topic before reading about it. In addition to activating background knowledge, each of these activities can serve to pique students' curiosity about a selection, prompting them to approach it with questioning minds.

Prereading activities are a critical part of the instructional cycle and should be used with the following purposes in mind:

- To build and/or activate students' background knowledge on topics or concepts contained in the book.
- To elicit from students their feelings and reactions to ideas and issues contained in the book before confronting those issues.
- To help students identify more intensely with characters.
- To set purposes for reading.
- To arouse students' curiosity and motivate them to read.

ANTICIPATION GUIDES

An anticipation guide (Readence, Bean, & Baldwin, 1981) is a list of statements with which the students are asked to agree or disagree. The statements are related to concepts, issues, or attitudes presented in the reading selection. Typically, three to five statements are used in an anticipation guide, and an effort is made to use statements that will result in differences of opinion and thus lead to discussion and debate.

The following steps may be used to develop and use an anticipation guide:

1. Identify major themes or ideas in the reading selection.
2. Write three to five statements related to selected themes or events that are likely to arouse discussion.
3. Present the statements to the students on an overhead projector, the chalkboard, or as a handout.
4. Allow a few minutes for students to respond privately to each statement by indicating their agreement or disagreement on paper.
5. Engage the students in a discussion about the statements by asking for their reactions. This discussion should include reasons for responses.

Asking students to take a stand on statements such as, "It's okay to disobey your parents," can generate lively discussion and allows students to explore and identify their own attitudes and beliefs as well as to listen to the ideas of peers prior to interacting with the author's or a character's attitudes on the issue. Generally, the discussion should begin with the teacher asking for a show of hands on the first statement, "How many of you agree with this statement?" "How many of you disagree?" All students are expected to indicate a response. Then the teacher may ask, "Of those of you who agreed, who can tell why you agreed with this statement?" Several students should be asked to give reasons. Then, "Those of you who disagreed, why did you do so?" Again, the teacher should allow as many children as possible to respond. Students should be provided opportunities to respond to their peers' comments. This format may be followed with each of the statements.

In addition to serving as vehicles for activating students' background knowledge and stimulating their curiosity, anticipation guides allow the teacher to discover students' attitudes and preconceived notions about book-related issues. Thus, they are a tool for assessing as well as for building and activating background knowledge.

Sample anticipation guides for several books are presented on the next few pages. A brief summary of each book is provided for the teacher and is not intended to be shared with the students. Actual student responses are offered in italics for two of the examples. It is important that the teacher remember that we are not suggesting that these are "correct" responses. They are provided here so the teacher can more fully understand the activity. Student responses will, and should, vary.

Example 2.1

- **Title:** *Fly Away Home*
- **Author:** Eve Bunting
- **Grade Level:** K–3
- **Summary:** A homeless young boy and his father live in the airport and move from location to location in order to avoid being noticed.

Anticipation Guide

Agree   **Disagree**

_____   _____   1. All people live in houses or apartments.

_____   _____   2. It would be easy to hide in an airport.

_____   _____   3. It is sad when people around you don't notice you.

Example 2.2

- **Title:** *The Book of the Pig*
- **Author:** Jack Denton Scott
- **Grade Level:** 4–6
- **Summary:** This book dispels many myths about pigs and provides much information about their activities, the variety of breeds, and the many ways they serve people.

Anticipation Guide

Agree   **Disagree**

_____   _____   1. Pigs are dirty animals.

_____   _____   2. Pigs serve no useful purpose.

_____   _____   3. Pigs are affectionate animals.

_____   _____   4. Pigs are stupid animals.

_____   _____   5. Pigs can be trained to do tricks.

_____   _____   6. Pigs are fussy about what they eat.

In addition to indicating their agreement or disagreement with statements in an anticipation guide, students may be asked to write a brief comment in response to each statement, as in Example 2.3.

Example 2.3 ——————————————————

- **Title:**   *Dragonwings*
- **Author:**   Laurence Yep
- **Grade Level:**   5–8
- **Summary:**   An eight-year-old boy travels from China to the United States to be with his father whom he has never seen. There he confronts prejudice and discrimination as well as his own misperceptions about Americans. He watches his father struggle toward achieving his dream to fly. The story takes place in the early 1900s and was inspired by the actual account of a Chinese immigrant who built a flying machine in 1909.

Anticipation Guide

Agree   **Disagree**

___X___   _____   1. It would be exciting to move to a new country.
I think you'd see a lot of interesting things in another country.

_____   ___X___   2. Discrimination and prejudice often work both ways between immigrants and native peoples.
Usually the people already living in a country don't like newcomers, but newcomers want to be friends.

_____   ___X___   3. A father has a duty to always protect his children from harm.
Parents should take care of their children, but eventually children must take care of themselves.

___X___   _____   4. People should not spend energy working on unrealistic goals.
If it's unrealistic, it's stupid for someone to spend time on it. He should find another goal.

The anticipation guide shown in Example 2.3 was presented to graduate students before its purpose or its relationship to a piece of literature was explained. What ensued was a thoughtful and lengthy discussion. The participants thought about the ideas, related them to their own experiences, shared interpretations of and responses to the statements, and supported their viewpoints.

Completed anticipation guides may be saved for reconsideration after a selection has been read. The format of the anticipation guide can be easily changed to include a single column for anticipation responses in which students put a plus or a minus symbol (or a smiling or frowning face) indicating agreement or disagreement, and a second column for reaction responses. Students complete this second column after reading the selection. For instance, Example 2.3 may be rewritten as shown in Example 2.4.

Example 2.4 _____

Anticipation/Reaction Guide

Anticipation Reaction

Anticipation	Reaction	
+	−	1. It would be exciting to move to a new country.
−	+	2. Discrimination and prejudice often work both ways between immigrants and native peoples.
−	−	3. A father has a duty to always protect his children from harm.
+	−	4. People should not spend energy working on unrealistic goals.

Upon completing the activity the second time, students may discover that their attitudes have changed as a result of their reading. Such changes are intriguing to students and may be a stimulus for writing.

OPINIONNAIRES/QUESTIONNAIRES

Opinionnaires/questionnaires (Reasoner, 1976) are useful tools for helping readers examine their own values, attitudes, opinions, or related experiences before they interact with book characters. Constructing an opinionnaire/questionnaire is very much like constructing an anticipation guide. The teacher first identifies themes, ideas, or major events around which he or she wishes to focus his or her instruction. Then he or she generates a series of questions to tap students' opinions, attitudes, or past experiences related to those themes. Some items on the opinionnaires/questionnaires may be open-ended, whereas others may be more structured and offer students a checklist of possible responses.

Keep in mind that the purpose of this activity is to facilitate students' thinking about their own attitudes and experiences related to selected issues, not to elicit "correct" responses. Be accepting of students' honest responses and do not do what one student teacher we observed did. He continued to probe a student who made a comment apparently contrary to his own values until she finally changed her response. The student grew increasingly uncomfortable and it became obvious to the entire class that the teacher was trying to elicit a particular response. He was not truly interested in his students' opinions. Needless to say, the teacher's behavior served as a roadblock to the grand conversation that the activity could have prompted.

The opinionnaire/questionnaire depicted in Example 2.5 provides a structure for young children to talk about their experiences with stuffed animals. When they subsequently hear or read the story *The Velveteen Rabbit*, they are more likely to appreciate the story events. Note that extra spaces are included so that students may insert their own ideas. Examples 2.6 and 2.7 are intended for use with older children.

Example 2.5 _____

- ■ **Title:** *The Velveteen Rabbit*
- ■ **Author:** Margery Williams
- ■ **Grade Level:** 3–5
- ■ **Summary:** This is the story of a stuffed toy rabbit that becomes real.

Opinionnaire/Questionnaire

Do you have any stuffed animals?   yes ❏   no ❏

Which stuffed animal is your favorite?

What do you do with your stuffed animal?

_____   sleep with it

_____   keep it on a shelf

_____   take it to my friend's house and play with it

_____   take it on trips

_____   play school with it

_____   watch TV with it

_____   other   _____

_____

How long have you had it?

What did it look like when you first got it?

Does it look different now? How?

If it looks different now, why has it changed?

Example 2.6

- **Title:**   *The Bully of Barkham Street*
- **Author:**   Mary Stolz
- **Grade Level:**   4–6
- **Summary:**   Martin Hastings is a neighborhood bully who has few friends. He emerges as a sympathetic character who begins to make efforts to change his reputation.

Opinionnaire/Questionnaire

1. What words best describe a bully?

   _____ heroic   _____ wise guy   _____ mean

   _____ conceited   _____ unloved   _____ spoiled

   _____ babyish   _____ poor   _____ wealthy

   _____ _____   _____ _____   _____ _____

2. What do you think causes a person to become a bully?

   _____ He's just born that way.

   _____ Too many people have picked on him and made him mean.

   _____ He's a bully so he can get attention.

   _____ He thinks he's uglier than most people his age.

   _____ He's bigger than most people his age.

   _____ He's smaller than most people his age.

3. How would you recognize a bully?

   _____ From the way he brags

   _____ From the expression on his face

   _____ From the way he walks

   _____ From the way he talks

   _____ From the way he teases people

   _____ _____

   _____ _____

4. How would you cure a bully?

   _____ With love and kindness

   _____ With strict rules and punishment

   _____ By giving him a taste of his own medicine

   _____ By getting a meaner bully to frighten him

   _____ _____

   _____ _____

Note: This example was condensed from Reasoner (1972).

Reasoner (1972) suggested that students use the opinionnaire/questionnaire to poll others (students in other classrooms, parents, etc.) to see what they believe. The data may then be compiled for class summary and evaluation.

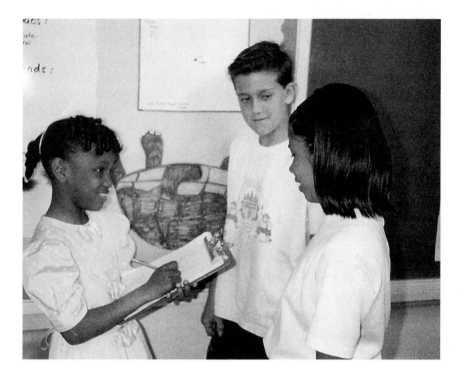

Example 2.7

- **Title:** *Roll of Thunder, Hear My Cry*
- **Author:** Mildred Taylor
- **Grade Level:** 6–8
- **Summary:** Set in the south during the Depression, this story relates the struggles of a black family and its encounters with hate and prejudice.

Opinionnaire/Questionnaire

Listed below are a few incidents that make some people feel bad.
Which of them would make you feel bad?

_____ when someone you love is ashamed of you

_____ when people call you names

_____ when people act as if they are better than you

_____ when you are punished for something you did that you should not have done

_____ when someone stares at you

_____ _____

_____ _____

_____ _____

What would you do if you were tricked out of a favorite possession by someone you knew?

_____ cry

_____ tell your parents and ask for their help

_____ tell that person's parents and ask for their help

_____ tell all your friends so they won't be nice to that person

_____ get it back somehow

_____ pretend you didn't like the possession anyway

_____ decide you didn't deserve the possession

_____ trick that person out of something to show him or her how it feels

_____ _____

_____ _____

If you were in a store and the clerk who was waiting on you
stopped helping you and turned to assist two other people, what
would you do?

_____ wait patiently

_____ leave and go somewhere else

_____ leave and tell your parents

_____ complain to the manager

_____ demand that the clerk finish helping you

_____ _____

A boy in your class is always bothering you, acting smarter than you, and getting into mischief. Which of the following describe what you would do?

_____ feel sorry for him

_____ try to be his friend and help him change

_____ ignore him

_____ beat him up

_____ hope someone catches him someday

_____ tell on him

_____ _____

_____ _____

If he came to you for help, what would you do?

_____ tell him "No way!"

_____ help him

_____ laugh at him

_____ pretend you'd help him, then don't

_____ _____

_____ _____

As with the anticipation guides, opinionnaires/questionnaires may be distributed again after students have read the book. Students may examine whether their answers have changed, and if so, why they have changed.

CONTRAST CHARTS

Contrast charts may also be used to facilitate students' thinking about ideas prior to encountering them in a story. They are very simple to develop, requiring only that the teacher identify theme-related contrasting categories under which students can list ideas. For example, in the book *Island of the Blue Dolphins*, by Scott O'Dell, Karana is left alone on an island for years and must learn to deal with loneliness. To tap students' feelings about and experiences with loneliness before they encounter Karana's feelings, the teacher might ask students to generate a list of times when they feel lonely and times when they do not feel lonely.

Contrast charts can be generated by the class as a whole, by small groups of children, or by individuals. We encourage the use of small groups with this activity. One student may act as recorder while three or four others contribute ideas to be written on the chart. Then each group can share its list with the entire class.

Example 2.8 ───────────────────────

- **Title:** *Frog and Toad are Friends*
- **Author:** Arnold Lobel
- **Grade Level:** K–2
- **Summary:** Frog and Toad, the best of friends, have many adventures together.

Contrast Chart

Some people are good to have as friends and some people aren't. List some of the qualities that are important to you in a good friend. Then list qualities that make a person a bad friend.

Good Friend	**Bad Friend**
1. *shares with you*	1. *tells your secrets to others*
2. *is nice*	2. *doesn't share*
3. *gives you things*	3. *won't play with you*
4.	4.
5.	5.
6.	6.

Example 2.9 ───────────────────────

- **Title:** *Alexander and the Terrible, Horrible, No Good, Very Bad Day*
- **Author:** Judith Viorst
- **Grade Level:** K–3
- **Summary:** Alexander has a horrible day when one thing after another goes wrong for him.

Contrast Chart

Have you ever heard people say, "That made my day!" or "That ruined my day"? They are referring to events that happened that make them feel especially good or particularly miserable and cranky. List some things that could happen to you that could make your day either good or bad.

Good Day	Bad Day
1.	1.
2.	2.
3.	3.
4.	4.
5.	5.
6.	6.

Students easily generate ideas for the chart in Example 2.9. They then are quite sympathetic with Alexander's misadventures and usually become very excited if Alexander confronts one of the very events that they listed as making their own day a bad one.

In Example 2.10 children respond to the idea of moving. This move could be from one country to another (as the character experiences), one house to another, or one classroom to another. By asking children to think about the positive and negative aspects of moving, teachers are setting the stage for students to understand the character's mixed feelings of joy and loss.

Example 2.10

- **Title:** *Grandfather's Journey*
- **Author:** Allen Say
- **Grade Level:** 2 and up
- **Summary:** A Japanese-American man tells the story of his grandfather's move to America and of his feelings of love and longing for both his native country and his adopted country.

Contrast Chart

Good Things about Moving	Bad Things about Moving
1.	1.
2.	2.
3.	3.
4.	4.
5.	5.
6.	6.

Example 2.11

- **Title:** *Stuart Little*
- **Author:** E. B. White
- **Grade Level:** 4–6
- **Summary:** This story tells the humorous adventures of a two-inch mouse who is born into a human family.

Contrast Chart

What would it be like if you were two inches tall? List some things that would be difficult to do. List some things that would be easy to do.

Difficult	Easy
1.	1.
2.	2.
3.	3.
4.	4.
5.	5.
6.	6.

Children find this book very entertaining. They are amused as Stuart's size becomes advantageous at certain times and quite a problem at others. Some of the incidents the students are sure not to anticipate!

SEMANTIC MAPS

Semantic maps are graphic displays of categorized information. They may be used to build vocabulary and to activate and organize students' background knowledge on a given topic (Johnson & Pearson, 1984; Johnson, Pittelman, & Heimlich, 1986). They give students anchor points to which new concepts they will encounter can be attached (McNeil, 1987). To make a semantic map, the teacher first writes and encircles a term that is central to the reading selection on the chalkboard. In a selection about schools, for example, the teacher might write the word "school" in the middle of the chalkboard. He or she next generates categories related to the central concept. For our school example, he or she might write "rooms," "people," and "studies." Each is encircled and lines are drawn from the categories to the central concept of "school" to indicate a relationship. Then the teacher elicits from the students exemplars, details, or subordinate ideas for each of the categories. Within the category of "people," for example, the students may list "children," "teachers," "principal," and so on. These terms are written in the category circles. The teacher leads the students in a discussion about the terms and their relationships. Research suggests that this discussion is key to the effectiveness of the technique (Stahl & Vancil, 1986). Once a map is generated, the class may want to save it to refer to during or after reading. At any point the map may be modified to reflect new information or ideas.

Another way to develop a semantic map is to have the students brainstorm and record the subordinate ideas after being told the central concept and then to group them into categories and label the categories. This approach is similar to Taba's (1967) list-group-label technique for concept development.

The use of semantic maps prior to reading has been found to result in better story recall in low-ability readers than the use of the more traditional directed reading technique in which new content, new vocabulary, and the purpose for reading a selection are discussed prior to reading (Sinatra, Stahl-Gemake, & Berg, 1984). The use of semantic maps is supported by schema theory described in Chapter One. Schemata (plural of schema) are networks of knowledge that readers' store in their minds. Semantic maps help students tap those networks, integrate new information, and restructure existing networks.

Example 2.12

- **Title:** *Peppe the Lamplighter*
- **Author:** Elisa Bartone
- **Grade Level:** K–3
- **Summary:** Young Peppe wants to help support his family and accepts a job as the lamplighter in Little Italy, a New York City neighborhood. His father, initially upset about Peppe's choice of work, ultimately is proud of his son.

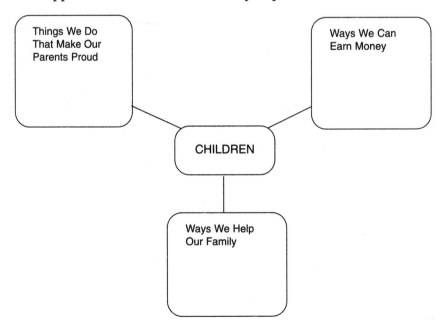

Example 2.13 _____

- **Title:** *Island of the Blue Dolphins*
- **Author:** Scott O'Dell
- **Grade Level:** 4–6
- **Summary:** This is the story of Karana, an Indian girl, who survives alone on an island for eighteen years.

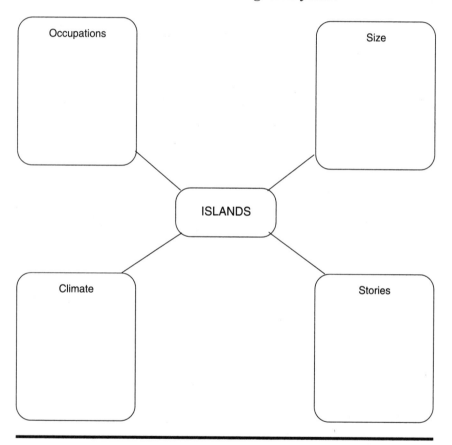

Example 2.14 _____

- **Title:** *In the Year of the Boar and Jackie Robinson*
- **Author:** Bette Lord
- **Grade Level:** 4–6
- **Summary:** This book tells the story of an immigrant family's experiences in the United States.

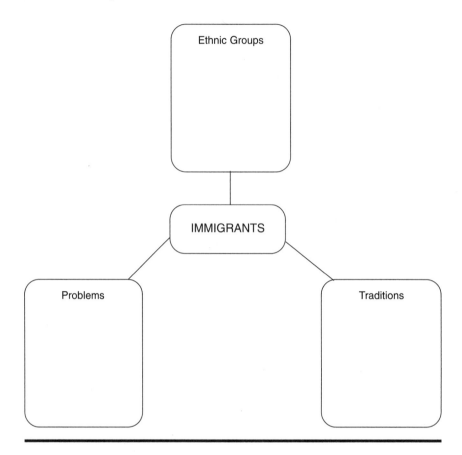

KWL CHARTS

Another activity that helps students access their background knowledge on a given subject is the KWL (know, want to know, learned) chart developed by Ogle (1986). The KWL chart is intended to be used before and then after reading or listening to a selection that contains some factual content. Prior to interacting with the selection, the students brainstorm and write on a chart all they know about a given concept. In a second column, students record what they would like to know about the topic. For example, prior to reading the poem "Honeybees" in *Joyful Noise*, by Paul Fleischman, students would record everything they know about honeybees in one column and what they want to know in a second column, as in Example 2.15. By identifying questions, students develop their reasons for reading, and as a result are more likely to be actively engaged in the reading process.

Example 2.15 _____

- **Title:** "Honeybees" from *Joyful Noise*
- **Author:** Paul Fleischman
- **Grade Level:** K–6
- **Summary:** This poem, one of a collection of poems about insects, describes the activities of the queen and worker honeybees.

KWL Chart
Honeybees

What we know	What we want to know
make honey	*How is the queen different?*
live in hives	*Who lays the eggs?*
have a queen	*How many are laid at a time?*
sting	*How far away do bees fly from their hives?*
	Why does the sting hurt so much?

Once the selection has been read, students record in a third column what they have learned about the topic as a result of having read the selection. In addition, any information listed in the first column that was inaccurate should be corrected.

Example 2.16 _____

- **Title:** *Ox-Cart Man*
- **Author:** Donald Hall
- **Grade Level:** K–3
- **Summary:** Everyday life of one New England family living in the early nineteenth century is depicted over the course of a year in this beautifully illustrated book.

KWL Chart
Life in Nineteenth-Century New England

What we know	**What we want to know**	**What we learned**
no cars	*What kind of work did people do?*	*walked long distances to a marketplace*
no telephones	*With no cars, how did they travel?*	*used candles for light*
not many people	*Was life very different from ours?*	*everyone in the family worked hard*
		saved feathers from geese
		cooked over a fire
		got syrup from maple trees
		they did the same things year after year

Example 2.17

- **Title:** *Is This a House for Hermit Crab?*
- **Author:** Megan McDonald
- **Grade Level:** K–2
- **Summary:** A hermit crab has outgrown his shell and searches for a larger one.

KWL Chart
Hermit Crabs

What we know	**What we want to know**	**What we learned**

It is important that the teacher restrict use of this activity to books that contain accurate information. Do not ask students what they know and what they have learned about whales from a work of fiction that presents whales that chat with one another and have cute personalities. The wonderful story of *Gilberto and the Wind*, by Marie Hall Ets, anthropomorphizes the wind, using phrases such as "Wind likes my soap bubbles" and "Wind is all tired out" that clearly are inappropriate to include on a knowledge chart. Therefore, the activity should not be used with this particular book.

By no means, however, should this activity be restricted to use with predominantly informational texts. Many works of fiction have considerable content that students often do not realize they are learning. In *Johnny Tremain*, by Esther Forbes, students learn a great deal about the Revolutionary War. In *Sadako and the Thousand Paper Cranes*, by Eleanor Coerr, students learn about leukemia. In *Where the Red Fern Grows*, by Wilson Rawls, students learn about life in the Ozarks. In *Miracles on Maple Hill*, by Virginia Sorensen, students learn about the production of maple syrup. The teacher must be familiar with the reading selection and be confident that information presented about a concept under consideration is accurate before using it in a KWL chart.

It is likely that a number of questions generated by the students will not be addressed by the reading selection. Students should be encouraged to pursue other sources of information. Ogle (1986) says that this helps students recognize the "priority of their personal desire to learn over simply taking in what the author has chosen to include" (p. 567). She suggests adding a fourth column (KWLH) in which students suggest how they will obtain the information (D. Ogle, personal communication, December 2, 1994), as in Example 2.18.

An additional modification of this versatile chart includes a column on affect (KWLA) to be completed after reading (Mandeville, 1994). Students may use this column to respond personally to the information they have learned, indicating what they find most interesting in the selection, identifying parts in the reading they liked the best or least, or noting why some information is particularly important to them. As with each of the strategies mentioned in this book, discussion is important, particularly when personal reactions are called for. Remember that the teacher may need to model personal responses for the students several times before expecting students to be willing to react personally to the content and share their reactions with peers. This linking of affective and cognitive domains has tremendous potential to spark students' interest in the factual information presented in many books, and Mandeville (1994) suggests that students who attach their own importance and personal relevance to information are likely to comprehend and remember the information better.

Example 2.18 _____

- **Title:**   *The Sign of the Beaver*
- **Author:**   Elizabeth Speare
- **Grade Level:**   4–6
- **Summary:**   A young boy learns a great deal about Indians who help him after he is separated from his family.

KWLH Chart
Indians

What we know	What we want to know	What we learned	How we'll find out more

Example 2.19 _____

- **Title**   *Summer of the Swans*
- **Author:**   Betsy Byars
- **Grade:**   7–8
- **Summary:**   This is the story of the relationship between a girl and her retarded brother.

KWLA Chart
Retardation

What we know	What we want to know	What we learned	What we feel about it

---

CONCLUSION

The five prereading activities described in this chapter encourage students' participation and interest in the literature, build or activate students' background knowledge, help students think about their beliefs and attitudes related to issues in a reading selection, and help students identify with characters. Anticipation guides, opinionnaires/questionnaires, contrast charts, semantic maps, and KWL charts involve students in thinking, responding, exploring, and shaping ideas. Students are allowed the opportunity to examine their own beliefs, experiences, and knowledge as well as those of their classmates. It is hoped that the students will find the literature personally meaningful after engaging in these activities and that they will approach ideas contained in the books with greater interest, purpose, and appreciation.

REFERENCES

Bartone, E. (1993). *Peppe the lamplighter*. New York: Lothrop, Lee & Shepard.

Bunting, E. (1991). *Fly away home*. New York: Clarion.

Byars, B. (1981). *Summer of the swans*. New York: Penguin.

Coerr, E. (1977). *Sadako and the thousand paper cranes*. New York: Putnam.

Ets, M. (1963). *Gilberto and the wind*. New York: Scholastic.

Fleischman, P. (1988). *Joyful noise*. New York: HarperTrophy.

Forbes, E. (1971). *Johnny Tremain*. New York: Dell.

Hall, D. (1979). *Ox-cart man*. New York: Penguin.

Johnson, D. & Pearson, P. v D. (1984). *Teaching reading vocabulary* (2nd ed.). New York: Holt, Rinehart, & Winston.

Johnson, D., Pittelman, S., & Heimlich, J. (1986). Semantic mapping. *The Reading Teacher, 39,* 778–783.

Lobel, A. (1970). *Frog and toad are friends*. New York: Scholastic.

Lord, B. (1984). *In the year of the boar and Jackie Robinson*. New York: Harper Junior Books.

Mandeville, T. F. (1994). KWLA: Linking the affective and cognitive domains. *The Reading Teacher, 47,* 679–680.

McDonald, M. (1990). *Is this a house for hermit crab?* New York: Orchard.

McNeil, J. (1987) *Reading comprehension: New directions for classroom practice* (2nd ed.). Glenview, IL: Scott, Foresman.

O'Dell, S. (1960). *Island of the blue dolphins*. New York: Dell.

Ogle, D. (1986). K-W-L: A teaching model that develops active reading of expository text. *The Reading Teacher, 39,* 564–570.

Rawls, W. (1961). *Where the red fern grows*. New York: Doubleday.

Readence, J., Bean, T., Baldwin, R. (1981). *Content area reading: An integrated approach*. Dubuque, IA: Kendall/Hunt.

Reasoner, C. (1972). *Where the readers are*. New York: Dell.

Reasoner, C. (1976). *Releasing children to literature* (revised ed.). New York: Dell.

Say, A. (1993). *Grandfather's journey*. Boston: Houghton Mifflin.

Scott, J. D. (1981). *The book of the pig*. New York: G. P. Putnam's Sons.

Sinatra, R., Stahl-Gemake, J., & Berg, D. (1984). Improving reading comprehension of disabled readers through semantic mapping. *The Reading Teacher, 38,* 22–29.

Sorensen, V. (1957). *Miracles on Maple Hill*. New York: Harcourt Brace & World.

Speare, E. (1983). *The sign of the beaver*. Boston: Houghton Mifflin.

Stahl, S. & Vancil, S. (1986). Discussion is what makes semantic maps work in vocabulary instruction. *The Reading Teacher, 40,* 62–67.

Stolz, M. (1977). *The bully of Barkham Street*. New York: Dell.

Taba, H. (1967). *Teachers handbook for elementary social studies*. Reading, MA: Addison-Wesley.

Taylor, M. (1983). *Roll of thunder, hear my cry*. Toronto: Bantam.

Viorst, J. (1972). *Alexander and the terrible, horrible, no good, very bad day*. New York: Atheneum.

White, E. B. (1973). *Stuart Little*. New York: Harper & Row.

Williams, M. (1975). *The velveteen rabbit*. New York: Camelot.

Yep, L. (1975). *Dragonwings*. New York: Harper Junior Books.

CHAPTER THREE

During-Reading Activities

During Reading

Purposes	Activities
■ To facilitate comprehension	■ Literature maps
■ To focus attention	■ Character maps
■ To encourage reactions to ideas	■ Character webs
	■ Journals
■ To call attention to language	■ Feelings charts
	■ Contrast charts
■ To allow for personal responses	

A lthough there will be many occasions when teachers will wish to introduce a book and then let the children read it uninterrupted, during directed literature experiences, they will want to provide activities that will enhance students' understanding of the selection or focus their attention on particular themes, issues, characters, or events. Furthermore, teachers will want to provide activities that will prompt students to react to ideas, events, or characters or to identify what they find interesting or meaningful. In other words, they will want to enhance the interactions between the students and the text.

Rosenblatt (1978) referred to these interactions between readers and texts as *transactions* in order to emphasize the dynamic relationship between the two. She argued that readers infuse intellectual and emotional meanings into the patterns of symbols we call words and that "the special meanings and associations that words in a book have for each reader will determine what the work communicates to him [or her]" (p. 25). She stated that an important task for the teacher is to foster fruitful transactions between the reader and the text. One way to do this is to provide an environment in which students are allowed to respond personally to works of literature and to explore and compare their responses to those of classmates.

Several of the activities presented in this chapter, indeed in this book, provide these opportunities. Students are encouraged to bring themselves to the literary experience and respond personally to the text. They are encouraged to listen to the points of view of others and are given opportunities to reflect on and analyze their own responses. In addition, some of these activities are excellent tools for calling students' attention to effective use of language. As noted in Chapter One, one of the advantages of using literature in the classroom is that it provides a rich language model.

This chapter describes six activities in which teachers may engage children during reading. *Literature maps* enhance students' comprehension by assisting them in identifying and organizing information they find important or interesting. Literature maps can be used to focus students' attention on text elements, such as setting and characters, to call attention to language, and to allow for personal responses. *Character maps* are used specifically for analyzing characters and their evolving relationships. *Character webs* also may be used to analyze characters. They differ from character maps in that they require the students to record specific behaviors to support identified character traits. Several *journal* formats are described in this chapter, all of which promote reactions and personal responses to reading selections. *Feelings charts* facilitate comprehension by providing a format for identifying and describing different viewpoints. *Contrast charts*, described in Chapter Two as a prereading activity, are appropriate for all phases of the instructional cycle, and they are included here so the reader may see examples of their application in another context and therefore gain a greater appreciation of their flexibility.

In summary, activities in this chapter are designed to:

- Facilitate students' comprehension.
- Focus students' attention on particular themes, issues, or characters.
- Encourage students to react to ideas, events, and characters.
- Call students' attention to effective uses of language.
- Allow students to identify what they find most meaningful in a reading selection.

Like the prereading activities described in Chapter Two, the activities discussed in this chapter require a response from each student and allow every student to experience success.

LITERATURE MAPS

Literature maps, described by Haskell (1987), provide a means for responding to literature while reading. Literature maps are constructed by folding a piece of paper (8 ½-by-11 inches or larger) into four or more sections and labeling each section with a category name. Categories may include "setting," "themes," "predictions," "vocabulary," "questions," "symbols," "imagery," or the "names of characters." Categories are generally identified by the teacher. However, some students may like to create their own categories as they are reading.

The reader's task is to write category-related information in each section as he or she reads a chapter or a book. For example, given a section labeled "setting," the reader jots down words, phrases, or sentences about the setting of the story. It is not necessary for the student to record all data regarding a particular category. Rather, each student may include what he or she considers the most interesting or important information. A category such as "language" will yield diverse responses from students. Some students will write expressions they think are funny or unusual. Others may record words or phrases that confuse them. Still others may write descriptive phrases. As children bring their individuality to the literature, they will respond differently from one another.

Once the maps have been completed by individual students, they are shared. The teacher draws a large map on the chalkboard and asks the students to contribute responses from their personal maps to the class map. Students may modify their personal maps while creating the class map.

As Haskell (1987) pointed out, the benefits of this activity are many. First, students become more actively involved in their reading. They paraphrase ideas and identify important or interesting information while they are reading. Second, discussion is enhanced. Because children have taken notes while reading, they are better prepared to discuss the traits or behaviors of a particular character, for example. Third, the students have a record to which they may refer when writing about the reading selection. Fourth, students have the opportunity to hear what their peers think is important or interesting. Fifth, students begin to notice language that is appealing or effective. They begin to comment, "I like the way the author described that"—a first step toward internalizing and modeling effective language. Sixth, a map may be constructed at several points in a book, and students can trace the development of the plot or of characters.

An additional and very important benefit of this activity is that all students can contribute to the class map and feel success as their ideas are included. For example, given a particular character, some students will simply respond with physical characteristics such as "has red hair" or "is 5 years old," while other students may generate higher-level responses such as "is considerate of others," "is a listener," or "appears to have a good self-concept." All levels of responses should be accepted by the teacher. Thus, all students will feel comfortable responding and should have something to contribute to the classroom map and follow-up discussion. When a higher-level response is given, the teacher should ask, "What makes you think so?" The student then must draw on incidents from the reading selection that led to his or her conclusions. By verbalizing his or her reasons, the student is modeling his or her thinking patterns for other students.

It is important that the teacher not overwhelm the students with too many categories. Further, the teacher must recognize that some students may find this activity disruptive to their reading, particularly if they feel the need to stop quite frequently to record information. We recommend that students who find this activity too disruptive be allowed to listen to or read a selection in its entirety first, then complete the literature map during a second reading.

Example 3.1

- **Title:** *Ramona and Her Father*
- **Author:** Beverly Cleary
- **Grade Level:** 3–5
- **Summary:** Ramona's father loses his job, Ramona and Beezus go on a campaign to help him quit smoking, and Ramona practices acting so she can get a job on television commercials and earn enough money to help support her family.

Literature Map

Ramona	Her Father
happy	*lost his job*
making Christmas list	*worried*
loves gummy bears	*no fun anymore*
wants to help family	*patient*
practices commercials	*no money*
gets burs in hair	
Beezus	**Questions**
grouchy	*Will her father get another job?*
loves gummy bears	*Will her father be fun again?*
going through a phase	*Will Ramona be in commercials?*

Example 3.2

- **Title:**   *Child of the Silent Night: The Story of Laura Bridgman*
- **Author:**   Edith Fisher Hunter
- **Grade Level:**   5–6
- **Summary:**   This is the true story of Laura Bridgman, who became blind and deaf at a very early age, and the successful efforts of her friends and teachers to educate her and enable her to communicate with those around her.

Literature Map

Setting	Laura
Uncle Asa	**Laura's parents**

Literature maps may be used at any grade level. A kindergarten teacher may modify the activity by using only the large class map. Before reading the book he or she may tell the students to pay particular attention to two of the characters or to the setting: category names that are written on the board. The teacher then reads the story, stopping periodically to ask the students if anything can be written in any of the categories. "Can we write anything about Little Red Riding Hood yet?" Students' responses are recorded and the activity continues. Recording in writing should be done even with nonreaders. It is good modeling of the function of print and helps to establish the link between oral and written language. The teacher may conclude the activity by reading all the student comments in each category and leading a discussion about the story.

Example 3.3

- **Title:** *Are You My Mother?*
- **Author:** P. D. Eastman
- **Grade Level:** K–1
- **Summary:**   A little bird breaks out of his shell while his mother is away searching for food. The baby bird sets off to find his mother and asks a variety of animals and vehicles if they are his mother before he is reunited with her.

Literature Map

Mother Bird	Baby Bird
cares about her baby *goes off to find food*	*breaks out of shell* *leaves nest and falls* *can't fly* *wants to find his mother*

Possible Mothers		Questions
kitten *hen* *dog* *cow*	*steam shovel* *plane* *boat* *car*	*Will the baby bird find his mother?* *Will the baby bird get hurt?* *Will the baby bird get lost?*

CHARACTER MAPS

Character maps may be used to help students recognize the traits of selected characters in a book, as well as relationships between characters. After the students have read part of the book, the teacher or the students identify at least two characters for analysis. Each character's name is placed near the top of a circle or box on a single piece of paper. Students then are asked to list character traits under each of the names. Thus, students may have several circles or boxes on a piece of paper, each with a name and list of traits underneath.

Next, the students draw an arrow from one character to another. Above and below the arrow, the students write words or phrases that tell how the first character feels about the second ("admires"), or what his or her relationship is to the second ("parent"). Several descriptors may be generated. A second arrow is drawn between these two characters, pointing in the opposite direction. Near this arrow the students write the second character's feelings about or relationship to the first.

Example 3.4

- **Title:** *Charlotte's Web*
- **Author:** E. B. White
- **Grade Level:** 3–6
- **Summary:** Charlotte is a clever spider who befriends a pig named Wilbur and with the help of other animals saves him from a sure death.

Character Map (During Chapter Four)

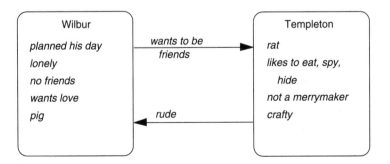

Character maps may be particularly useful in tracing the development of relationships. In the following example, two character maps are shown. The first was created by a class during the first part of the story. The second was written near the end of the story. These maps allow students to analyze the changes in characters as well as the changing relationships between characters.

Example 3.5

- **Title:** *Mike Mulligan and His Steam Shovel*
- **Author:** Virginia L. Burton
- **Grade Level:** K–2
- **Summary:** Mike Mulligan is sad because he and his steam shovel, Mary Anne, have been replaced by new, modern equipment. In order to find work, he goes to a neighboring town where he meets Henry B. Swap who intends to trick him into doing work for no pay. The story ends happily when Henry B. Swap appreciates Mike Mulligan's skills and stories.

Character Map (Story Beginning)

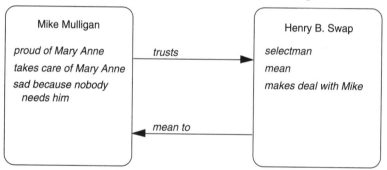

Character Map (Story Ending)

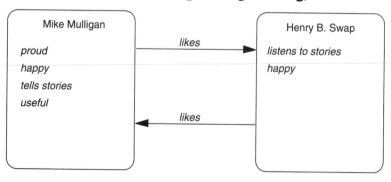

For more complex pieces of literature, several character maps might be developed. For example, in the book *Dragon's Gate*, by Laurence Yep, the young boy Otter greatly admires his Uncle Foxfire at the beginning of the book; is angry, bitter and disappointed with him later in the book; and then comes to understand and appreciate his uncle's courage and wisdom by the end of the book. The following three character maps illustrate changes that occur in the boy's perceptions of his uncle.

Example 3.6

- **Title:** *Dragon's Gate*

- **Author:** Laurence Yep

- **Grade Level:** 5 and up

- **Summary:** Otter, a young Chinese boy, flees his country to join his legendary Uncle Foxfire and his father in America as they acquire new skills and knowledge by working on the transcontinental railroad. They plan to use this knowledge when they return to China to conduct the "Great Work." Otter is surprised by the working conditions and prejudice he encounters.

Character Map (Chapters 1–4)

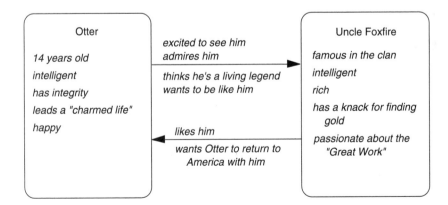

Otter		Uncle Foxfire
14 years old	excited to see him / admires him	famous in the clan
intelligent	thinks he's a living legend / wants to be like him	intelligent
has integrity		rich
leads a "charmed life"		has a knack for finding gold
happy	likes him / wants Otter to return to America with him	passionate about the "Great Work"

Character Map (Chapter 10)

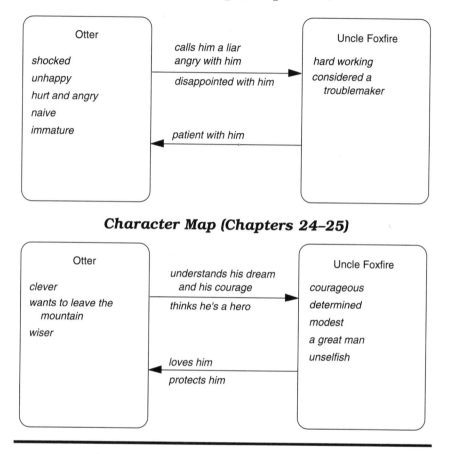

Otter		Uncle Foxfire
shocked	*calls him a liar*	hard working
unhappy	*angry with him*	considered a
hurt and angry	*disappointed with him*	troublemaker
naive		
immature	*patient with him*	

Character Map (Chapters 24–25)

Otter		Uncle Foxfire
clever	*understands his dream and his courage*	courageous
wants to leave the mountain	*thinks he's a hero*	determined
wiser		modest
	loves him	a great man
	protects him	unselfish

CHARACTER WEBS

Another strategy for analyzing characters is the character web. In this strategy, students identify character traits and cite examples from the text as evidence. Bromley (1991) notes that webbing enhances comprehension and learning, links reading and writing, and promotes enjoyment. Character webs draw readers back to the text as they look for supporting examples, and so their interactions with the text are enriched.

Webs are very flexible instructional tools, and there are a great variety of web types (Bromley, 1991). The examples included here have at the center the name of a character. Circles placed out from the center contain character traits. Shooting off from these circles are supporting facts or information drawn from the text. For example, in the book *Doctor DeSoto*, a character that might be analyzed is the doctor. Students might decide that he is clever, nice, cautious, and a good worker. After recording these traits in the circles, the students support their decisions by citing incidents from the story.

Example 3.7

- **Title:**   *Doctor DeSoto*
- **Author:**   William Steig
- **Grade Level:**   K–2
- **Summary:** A mouse dentist and his wife typically refuse to take dangerous animals as patients. However, when they are approached by a suffering fox, they make an exception. They discover that they had better protect themselves from being eaten, and devise a clever plan to outsmart the fox.

Example 3.8 _____

- **Title:** *Crazy Lady!*

- **Author:** Jane Leslie Conly

- **Grade Level:** 6 and up

- **Summary:** A boy whose life has changed after the death of his mother slowly befriends the local alcoholic and her retarded son.

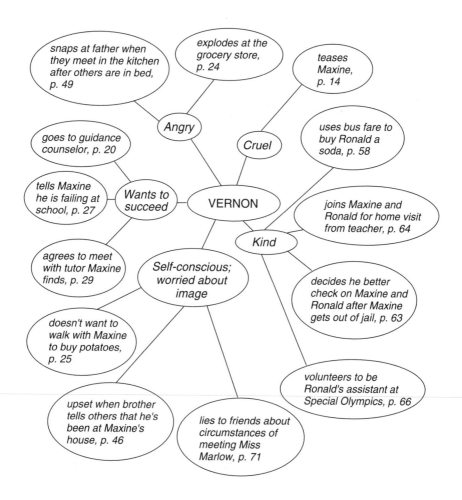

JOURNALS

Journals are a wonderful vehicle for integrating reading and writing. The act of writing in response to a reading selection helps to move both younger and older children beyond literal comprehension to a more complete understanding of the content of a book (Barone, 1989) and encourages personal, thoughtful engagement with books (Fuhler, 1994). There are many types of journals. Double-entry journals, reading logs, partner journals, and character journals will be described here.

The purpose of a double-entry journal is to allow students to select passages they find meaningful in a reading selection and then to write about why those passages are meaningful. Students may use 8½-by-11-inch lined paper that has been folded in half lengthwise. In the left-hand column, the student summarizes interesting information or copies verbatim a sentence or paragraph of his of her own choosing from the reading selection and records the page number. Directly across from the text information or quote, in the right-hand column, the student reacts to the passage. Selections and responses will vary widely. Some passages may be selected because they are funny or use interesting language. Others may be selected because they touch the student's heart or remind the student of experiences in his or her own life.

This activity encourages interaction between the selection and the students and gives each student a chance to identify what is meaningful to him or her. Students may choose to share their responses with one another or to keep them private. The double-entry journal may be used effectively with children as young as first graders (Barone, 1990).

Example 3.9 _____

- **Title:**   *The Art Lesson*
- **Author:**   Tomie dePaola
- **Grade Level:**   K–2
- **Summary:**   This is the story of little Tommy's desire to be an artist. His family and friends applaud and encourage his talent, but at school he finds out that the children are not allowed to use their own crayons or have more than one piece of paper.

Double-Entry Journal

Quote	Response
"Once Tommy took a flashlight and a pencil under the covers and drew pictures on his sheets."	*That's funny. I've heard of people using a flashlight to read under the covers but not to draw!*
"And I want you to take those birthday crayons home with you and leave them there."	*How mean. Tommy is excited about his crayons and he's a good drawer. That teacher should let him use his own crayons.*

Example 3.10

- **Title:** *Secrets of a Wildlife Watcher*
- **Author:** Jim Arnosky
- **Grade Level:** 3–6
- **Summary:** In this informational book, the author describes techniques for observing wildlife and provides interesting facts about many animals.

Double-Entry Journal

Interesting Information	Reaction or Related Experiences
Owls sometimes swallow their prey whole. They cough up undigestible bones and hair in the form of a pellet. (p. 13)	*Last year my teacher brought in owl pellets and we got to examine them. We found lots of bones in the pellets and were able to figure out that the owl had eaten a mouse.*
A deer has a four-compartment stomach and chews its cud. (p. 21)	*I knew that cows brought up food again and chewed their cud but I didn't realize that deer did this!*

Reading logs, or literature logs, are more structured than double-entry journals in that the teacher provides a prompt for writing following a period of sustained silent reading or a shared reading experience. Kelly and Farnan (1991) have argued that reading logs can be effective in promoting the critical thinking skills of analysis and evaluation and promoting personal interactions with text if the appropriate prompts are provided. Appropriate prompts are those that involve a reader's perception of, association with, or evaluation of the text. Kelly and Farnan provide a list of sixteen "reader-response" prompts, including the following: "What character was your favorite? Why?" "What character did you dislike? Why?" "Are you like any character in the story? Explain." "Does anything in this work remind you of your own life or something that happened to you?" "What was your first reaction to the story?" "If you were a teacher, would you read this book to your class?"

Each of these questions emphasizes the students' personal interpretations and interactions with the text. Non–reader-response prompts are those that focus exclusively on the text, such as "Tell me about your book." When the reader-response prompts were used with fourth-grade students, Kelly and Farnan found that students went beyond a literal response to the text and engaged in thinking that involved analysis of text from a variety of perspectives.

Example 3.11 _____

- **Title:** *Flip-Flop Girl*
- **Author:** Katherine Paterson
- **Grade Level:** 4 and up
- **Summary:** When Vinnie's father dies, her brother stops speaking, and her mother can't make ends meet, the family moves across the county to live with Vinnie's grandmother. This book tells the story of the pain a young girl experiences when everything in her life seems to go wrong, and the special friendship that develops with a classmate who saves her brother.

Reading Log

Prompt (after reading Chapter Two):

Does anything in this chapter remind you of something that has happened to you?

Response:

I guess I'm really lucky. I have been going to this school since kindergarten. I can just imagine how awful it would be to leave your friends and move to a new place. I wouldn't want to be brand-new in a school where everybody else already knows each other. Vinnie must feel terrible, especially with everything else that's going on in her life. And that Heather girl was mean. I'm glad that the teacher seems so nice.

Partner journals (sometimes referred to as dialogue journals) require students to interact with another person, often a peer. The students may react to a chapter after it is read or the teacher may offer prompts. Once the writing is completed, students exchange journals with a partner who responds to their comments. This exchange may occur immediately or after a day or two has elapsed. Partners may be anonymous, each student having a secret identification number or name, or may be known. If two classes are reading the same book, journals may be exchanged across classes. Partner journals stimulate purposeful communication, provide an opportunity for writing, and allow for feedback from peers (Bromley, 1989). Morgan and Albritton (1990) reported success with this activity with children as young as second graders and found that both the content and the form of student writing improved over time.

Parents can be included in the journal experience also. Fuhler (1994) describes an experience she had with her junior high students and their parents in which the parents were invited to read the same book as their children and to participate in a dialogue about the book through the use of a partner journal. She found that most parents were delighted to be involved in the activity, and she was impressed with the thoughtful responses made by both parents and students.

Example 3.12

- **Title:** *A Gathering of Days*
- **Author:** Joan Blos
- **Grade Level:** 4–6
- **Summary:** Written in journal format, this book tells the story of two years in the life of a nineteenth-century New England girl.

Partner Journal

Dear Journal Partner:

This book is so cool! I have a diary, but I'm not very good about writing in it. Do you suppose someone will want to publish it someday?! Who do you think "the phantom" is that she has seen twice now?

Your Partner

Dear Partner:

I don't know who the phantom is. The book tells about bound boys who should be returned when they run away. Do you suppose the phantom is a boy who ran away? I wonder if Aunt Lucy is going to end up marrying the father.

I don't have a diary, but I think it would be fun to write in one. You could tell secrets to your diary that you wouldn't dare tell anyone else!

Your Partner

In character journals, suggested by Hancock (1993), the students assume the voice of the main character in a book as they record their feelings about story events. Hancock argues that when students are encouraged "to step inside [a character's] mind and heart and compose a personal response from his [or her] point of view" (p. 42), a high level of involvement and identification is attained. Readers grow in their understanding of the actions, motives, and emotions of the character. Hancock found in working with her eighth-grade students that they also needed the opportunity to react from their own perspectives, however. Students' personal entries can be set off in parentheses to distinguish them from the voice of the main character. By thinking about story events from both the character's perspective and their own perspectives, students may gain insights into their own values and ideals, thus gaining a greater sense of their identities—adding a powerful dimension to this type of journal.

Example 3.13

- **Title:** *Shiloh*

- **Author:** Phyllis Reynolds Naylor

- **Grade Level:** 4–6

- **Summary:** A young boy growing up in West Virginia discovers that a neighbor is abusing a dog. In his efforts to save the dog, the boy struggles with a number of moral dilemmas.

Character Journal

Student entry (during Chapter Two):

I can't stand it. Dad's making me take this dog back to that mean Judd Travers. Poor dog. I can tell he ain't been treated right. I can't believe Dad says it's no mind of ours how Judd treats the dog. The dog is shaking, he's so scared. How can Dad do this? What if the dog were a kid? What would Dad do then? What can I do to convince him not to take the dog back?

(How awful. I don't understand how people can be mean to animals, or how other people can let them get by with it. I know my mom would let me help a mistreated animal! She loves animals.)

It is important that teachers emphasize communication when using journals or logs in the classroom. Teachers should not correct students' spelling, punctuation, or syntax. Instead, the teacher may model standard usage by responding in writing to the content of students' entries, as shown in Example 3.14. Students will begin to modify their own spellings to match the conventions used by the teacher (Bode, 1989). Yet because the focus is on the message, not the form, students will be freed to think about ideas. Responses should be nonjudgmental, encouraging, and thought stretching (Fuhler, 1994; Hancock, 1993).

Example 3.14 ————————————————

- **Title:** *Crow Boy*
- **Author:** Taro Yashima
- **Grade Level:** 2–3
- **Summary:** A young Japanese boy who does not fit in with his schoolmates is befriended by a teacher who takes the time to learn about the boy and values his unique experiences.

Journal

Student Entry:

I likt how the boy nu so meny cro sonds.

Teacher Response:

Yes! He made many different crow sounds. I wonder how he learned to do that.

————————————————

Journals provide readers with the opportunity to think about and share their feelings and thoughts about characters, events, and ideas throughout their reading of a book. They give students a voice in their reading, and allow them to collaborate with an author as they create meaning together (Fuhler, 1994). A variety of journal formats should be used throughout the course of a school year, because each type provides a different kind of experience for both the teacher and the student. Double-entry journals, reading logs, partner journals, and character journals are just four journal formats. Edwards (1991–92) describes several other exciting formats that she claims are useful in promoting critical thinking skills.

FEELINGS CHARTS

A feelings chart is useful in helping students analyze characters' reactions to one or more events in a piece of literature. The chart also may serve as a vehicle for comparing and contrasting characters and is beneficial in building vocabulary.

The teacher may begin the activity by identifying several events that occur in the reading selection and then listing the characters who are influenced by the event. Events are listed, as in Example 3.15, down the side of a chart. Characters are listed across the top of the chart. As the students read or listen to a selection, they are asked to describe each character's feelings at the time of each event. Their descriptions are written where the respective characters and the events intersect on the chart.

Example 3.15

- **Title:** *The Wave*
- **Author:** Margaret Hodges
- **Grade Level:** 2–3
- **Summary:** The people of a village in Japan are threatened by a destructive tidal wave. Only an old man who resides at the top of a hill sees the danger. He attempts to warn the villagers by burning his precious rice fields.

Feelings Chart

Events	Characters		
	Ojiisan	Tada	Villagers
The water was calm and the village children played in the gentle waves.	*content satisfied happy*	*glad happy playful*	*thankful secure lucky peaceful cheerful*
Ojiisan sets fire to the rice fields.	*awful bad sad worried*	*anxious puzzled curious upset horrified*	*excited surprised unlucky vengeful angry crazy*

The huge tidal wave strikes the beach.	*afraid* *hopeful* *thankful*	*scared* *afraid* *panic*	*scared* *frightened* *terrified* *afraid*
The villagers, Ojiisan, and Tada look down upon the empty beach where their village used to stand.	*successful* *relieved* *right*	*proud* *amazed*	*lucky* *thankful* *sad* *dazed* *forgiving* *grateful* *horrified* *amazed* *shocked*

This activity may be conducted on a large chart in the front of the classroom with the teacher directing the entire activity and the students participating in a whole-class discussion. Alternative patterns include the use of small groups, pairs of students, or even individuals who complete their own charts and then later share their responses with the entire class.

Three student teachers modeled an interesting approach to this activity in a university seminar. The student teachers displayed the chart identifying key events in the story in the front of the room and then read the book aloud, pausing after each event. At each pause, they distributed small sheets of paper to everyone in the class and directed those students sitting on the right side of the classroom to write a single word that described how Ojiisan felt at the time. Students in the center of the classroom each wrote a word describing how Tada felt, and those students on the left side of the classroom wrote a word describing the feelings of the villagers. Each member of the class was permitted to write only one word. Then students, one row at a time, were instructed to bring their paper to the chart and stick it on the chart in the appropriate place. (Self-sticking paper was used, which saved an enormous amount of time.) After all papers had been displayed, each contribution was read and discussed. The variety of words generated by the class was astounding, and the reaction from the students was one of interest and curiosity. The responses in Example 3.15 are a sampling of those given by the university students.

Some students may wish to include a column labeled "Me" so they have an opportunity to respond to the events as well.

Example 3.16

- **Poem:** Casey at the Bat
- **Book:** *The Family Book of Best Loved Poems* (David L. George, Ed.)
- **Poet:** Ernest Lawrence Thayer
- **Grade Level:** 5 and up
- **Summary:** Fans count on Casey to win the baseball game. When he strikes out, it is a sad day in the history of Mudville.

Feelings Chart

Events	Characters		
	Casey	The Crowd	Me
Casey steps up to bat.			
The umpire calls, "Strike Two!"			
Casey strikes out.			

CONTRAST CHARTS

Contrast charts were described in Chapter Two as a prereading activity. These charts also may be used during reading as a means for recording contrasting ideas or information in a selection as it is read. For example, students may list the pros and cons of an issue, the advantages and disadvantages of a course of action, or the two sides of an argument as they are described in the selection. Once information from the selection has been organized in this manner, the chart may serve as a guide for writing. In Example 3.17, children record a character's reasons for and against taking a teddy bear to a sleepover while they are reading or listening to the story.

Example 3.17

- **Title:** *Ira Sleeps Over*
- **Author:**   Bernard Waber
- **Grade Level:**   K–3
- **Summary:** Ira has been invited to spend the night at a friend's house. He is very excited until his sister asks him whether he plans to take along his teddy bear. Ira wrestles with this question because he doesn't want to appear baby-ish to his friend, but he has never slept without "TaTa."

Contrast Chart

Reasons Why Ira Should Take His Teddy Bear	Reasons Why Ira Should Not Take His Teddy Bear
He's never slept without it.	His friend will laugh at him.
They're going to tell scary stories.	He'll think Ira is a baby.
His friend's house is very dark.	His friend will laugh at the bear's name.

Example 3.18

- **Title:**   *Call of the Wild*
- **Author:**   Jack London
- **Grade Level:**   7 and above
- **Summary:**   Buck is a well-cared-for family dog who is removed from his comfortable home in the south to serve as sled dog in the Alaskan wilderness.

Contrast Chart

Life in the South	Life in the North
1.	1.
2.	2.
3.	3.
4.	4.
5.	5.

CONCLUSION

Literature maps, character maps, character webs, journals, feelings charts, and contrast charts may be used during reading as a means to facilitate comprehension and to focus attention on content or language. Perhaps even more importantly, several of these activities provide students with the opportunity to react to a literature selection from a personal point of view and to identify what they find most meaningful.

REFERENCES

Arnosky, J. (1983). *Secrets of a wildlife watcher.* New York: Lothrop, Lee & Shepard.

Barone, D. (1989). Young children's written responses to literature: The relationship between written response and orthographic knowledge. In S. McCormick & J. Zutell (Eds.), *Cognitive and social perspectives for literacy research and instruction* (pp. 371–379). Chicago: National Reading Conference.

Barone, D. (1990). The written responses of young children: Beyond comprehension to story understanding. *The New Advocate, 3*(1), 49–56.

Blos, J. W. (1979). *A gathering of days.* New York: Macmillan.

Bode, B. (1989). Dialogue journal writing. *The Reading Teacher, 42,* 568–571.

Bromley, K. (1989). Buddy journals make the reading-writing connection. *The Reading Teacher, 43,* 122–129.

Bromley, K. (1991). *Webbing with literature: Creating story maps with children's books.* Boston: Allyn and Bacon.

Burton, V. L. (1967). *Mike Mulligan and his steam shovel.* Boston: Houghton Mifflin.

Cleary, B. (1975). *Ramona and her father.* New York: Dell.

Conly, J. L. (1993). *Crazy lady!* New York: HarperCollins.

dePaola, T. (1989). *The art lesson.* New York: Trumpet.

Eastman, P. D. (1960). *Are you my mother?* New York: Beginner Books.

Edwards, P. (1991–92). Using dialectical journals to teach thinking skills. *Journal of Reading, 35,* 312–316.

Fuhler, C. (1994). Response journals: Just one more time with feeling. *Journal of Reading, 37,* 400–405.

Hancock, M. (1993). Character journals: Initiating involvement and identification through literature. *Journal of Reading, 37,* 42–50.

Haskell, S. (1987). Literature mapping. *The California Reader, 20,* 29–31.

Hodges, M. (1964). *The wave.* Boston: Houghton Mifflin.

Hunter, E. F. (1963). *Child of the silent night: The story of Laura Bridgman.* Boston: Houghton Mifflin.

Kelly, P., & Farnan, N. (1991). Promoting critical thinking through response logs: A reader-response approach with fourth graders. In J. Zutell & S. McCormick (Eds.), *Learner Factors/Teacher Factors: Issues in Literacy Research and Instruction.* Fortieth Yearbook of the National Reading Conference. Chicago: The National Reading Conference.

London, J. (1974). *Call of the wild.* New York: Simon & Schuster.

Morgan, R. & Albritton, J. D. (1990). Primary students respond to literature through partner journals. *The California Reader, 23,* 29–30.

Naylor, P. R. (1991). *Shiloh.* New York: Atheneum.

Paterson, K. (1994). *Flip-flop girl.* New York: Lodestar.

Rosenblatt, L. (1978). *The reader, the text, the poem: The transactional theory of the literary word.* Carbondale: Southern Illinois University Press.

Steig, W. (1982). *Doctor DeSoto.* New York: Farrar, Straus & Giroux.

Thayer, E. (1952). Casey at the bat. In David L. George (Ed.), *The family book of best loved poems* (pp. 411–412). Garden City, NY: Hanover House.

Waber, B. (1975). *Ira sleeps over.* Boston: Houghton Mifflin.

White, E. B. (1952). *Charlotte's web.* New York: Harper & Row.

Yashima, T. (1965). *Crow boy.* New York: Viking.

Yep, L. (1993). *Dragon's gate.* New York: HarperCollins.

CHAPTER FOUR

Postreading Activities

Postreading

Purposes

- To encourage reflection
- To facilitate analysis and synthesis
- To promote personal responses and connections to ideas, themes, and issues encountered in the book
- To extend comprehension
- To facilitate organization of information

Activities

- Polar opposites
- Literary report cards
- Plot organizers
- World wheels
- Venn diagrams
- Book charts
- Table talk

The postreading activities a teacher chooses for his or her students will have an impact on how students view the reading selection as well as the reading act. If students are asked to reflect on important ideas, to share reactions, to return to the book to achieve greater understanding, to make connections between what they have just learned and what they already knew, and to use what was learned in a personally meaningful way, the selection will be viewed as a source of enjoyment and/or information and will be long remembered. Reading will be viewed as a meaning-based activity. If, on the other hand, students are asked only to respond to a series of low-level questions, to work quietly, to prove that they can sequence events by numbering them on a worksheet, or to complete a crossword puzzle to reinforce vocabulary, then they are likely to view the selection as simply a vehicle for skills instruction. Reading will be perceived as a skills-based activity.

The postreading activities we provide in this chapter are intended to be in keeping with the reasons for using literature in the classroom: to promote enjoyment of reading and to stimulate thoughtful interaction with text. All of the activities encourage reflection on some aspect of the text, such as characters, important ideas or events, themes, issues, or concepts. Many facilitate analysis and synthesis of ideas and encourage students to create something new from what they have learned. Some provide a vehicle for integration of prior knowledge and new information and promote the extension of students' comprehension beyond the book itself by helping students make connections across books, authors, and with their own lives. The activities facilitate the organization of ideas and provide a structure for meaningful discussion in which all students may share their ideas and interpretations.

The first activity, *polar opposites*, gives students a framework for thinking about characters or concepts. It requires analysis of characters' behaviors in order to draw conclusions about traits. *Literary report cards* provide a motivating format for thinking about and discussing characters and their traits. *Plot organizers* provide a graphic means for organizing and analyzing the plot of a story. *World wheels* are a vehicle for summarizing and organizing information from books with multicultural themes. *Venn diagrams* facilitate comparisons between two or more characters, events, or books, or between a character and the readers themselves. *Book charts* are useful for examining several books by the same author or with the same theme. The *table talk* strategy provides a forum for students to think about characters from different books in the same activity.

Thus, the post reading activities presented in this chapter may be used to:

- Encourage reflection on ideas, themes, and issues encountered in the book.
- Facilitate analysis and synthesis of ideas.
- Promote personal responses and connections to ideas, themes, and issues encountered in the book.
- Extend comprehension beyond the immediate text.
- Facilitate organization of information.

POLAR OPPOSITES

This activity may be used to help students analyze characters in a reading selection by asking them to rate one or more characters on a variety of dimensions along three-, five-, or seven-point scales. It is most effective when students are asked to draw examples from the text to justify their responses. In other words, students may not simply rate a character as "passive" rather than "aggressive." They also must state why they believe that character to be passive, citing incidents from the selection.

To develop a polar opposites guide, the teacher should begin by selecting a character and developing a list of qualities or characteristics that describe him or her. Then the teacher thinks of the opposite of each of those qualities. For example, if a character is very sure of himself, has many friends, and is easily angered, the list might include "confident," "popular," and "hot-tempered." Opposites of these might be "unsure," "unpopular," and "easygoing." (Opposites used will depend on the precise meaning intended by the initial term.) Each pair of opposites makes up its own continuum, as seen in the examples that follow. After reading a selection, students are asked to rate the character(s) by placing a mark on each continuum. In Example 4.1, we have placed an *X* on each continuum to show possible student responses. Please keep in mind that responses will vary.

Example 4.1 ⎯⎯⎯⎯⎯⎯⎯⎯⎯⎯⎯⎯⎯⎯⎯⎯⎯⎯⎯

- **Poem:** "The Road Not Taken"
- **Book:** *You Come Too* (Robert Frost)
- **Poet:** Robert Frost
- **Grade Level:** 4 and up
- **Summary:** A traveler reflects on his decision to take a less traveled road.

Polar Opposites

The traveler was

thoughtful	_X_	___	___	___	___	impulsive
timid	___	___	___	_X_	___	courageous
disappointed	___	___	___	_X_	___	content
realistic	___	_X_	___	___	___	unrealistic
a follower	___	___	___	___	_X_	a leader

Nowhere in the poem does the poet explicitly state that the traveler is thoughtful or impulsive, timid or courageous, disappointed or content, and so on. Students must examine the traveler's behaviors and thoughts in order to form a judgment. We have used this particular polar opposites activity with many groups and find it leads to considerable discussion and analysis of the poet's language.

Students must justify their responses in discussions or they may be asked to write or dictate to the teacher the reasons for their rating, as in Example 4.2. This example is from a primary-level book. Older students may need considerably more space between each continuum. It is important to remember that any rating is acceptable as long as the student is able to support his or her response with information from the text.

Note that in Example 4.2 a three-point scale rather than a five-point scale is used. *The Story of Ferdinand* is likely to be used with kindergarten children who may have difficulty with a five-point scale. The teacher must decide how many points to include on a polar opposites scale based on his or her knowledge of the students.

Example 4.2

- **Title:** *The Story of Ferdinand*
- **Author:** Munro Leaf
- **Grade Level:** K–1
- **Summary:** Ferdinand the bull is very different from other bulls. He is big and strong, but he is not interested in butting heads and fighting. He prefers to sit and smell flowers.

Polar Opposites

Ferdinand is

    happy   _X_   ____   ____   sad

He seems to be very happy as long as he can sit and smell flowers. He was even happy in the bull's ring because he could smell the flowers in the ladies' hair.

    healthy   _X_   ____   ____   unhealthy

He is big and strong which means he must be healthy.

    fierce   ____   ____   _X_   tame

Ferdinand likes to sit. He is not interested in fighting.

    same   ____   ____   _X_   different

Ferdinand is different from other bulls. He is happy sitting while the others like to fight and butt heads. He was not interested in being picked for the bull's ring. Other bulls did try hard to be picked.

brave   __X__   _____   _____   fearful

He must be fairly brave because he did what he wanted to do even though it was not like other bulls. Also, he did not seem upset about going into the bull's ring.

A modification of a polar opposites guide is presented in Example 4.3. In *From the Mixed-Up Files of Mrs. Basil E. Frankweiler*, two characters have contrasting traits and so may be rated along the same dimensions. Students are to write a "C" for Claudia and a "J" for Jamie at the appropriate point on each of the continua.

Example 4.3

- **Title:**   *From the Mixed-Up Files of Mrs. Basil E. Frankweiler*
- **Author:**   E. L. Konigsburg
- **Grade Level:**   5–6
- **Summary:**   Two children, Claudia and Jamie, run away from home and hide in a museum where they solve a mystery.

Polar Opposites

tightwad	_J_	_____	_____	_C_	big spender
cautious	_____	_C_	_J_	_____	adventurous
predictable	_____	_C_	_____	_J_	spontaneous
messy	_J_	_____	_____	_C_	neat and tidy
organized	_C_	_____	_____	_J_	disorganized

Polar opposites may be used successfully with all age groups to facilitate readers' reflection on characters in a piece of literature. They offer a structure for conducting discussions and can serve as a prewriting activity for a paper on character analysis. They encourage critical thinking, as students must analyze and synthesize what they know about a character in order to make judgments.

LITERARY REPORT CARDS

Literary report cards provide children with an entertaining vehicle for analysis of characters. In this activity, suggested by Johnson and Louis (1987), students are given the opportunity to issue grades to characters in a reading selection. Initially, the teacher may select the "subjects" on which the characters will be graded. Rather than academic areas, characters may be graded on personality traits, such as "courageous" or "patient." (Eventually, the students may be asked to generate the subject areas. Selection of subject areas requires higher-level thinking, as the students must reflect on the character, analyze his or her qualities and behavior, and label the qualities.) In addition to awarding the grades, students must comment on or cite evidence for each grade. Report cards themselves may be modeled after real report cards used at the school that the students attend.

Example 4.4 _____

- **Title:** *The Indian in the Cupboard*
- **Author:** Lynn Reid Banks
- **Grade Level:** 5–8
- **Summary:** When Omri puts a plastic Indian toy into a cupboard, it becomes a real live person. This book tells the story of Omri's adventures with the Indian and relates what an enormous responsibility it is to take care of another person.

Literary Report Card

S.M. All Elementary School

Student: Omri

Area	Grade	Comment
arts and crafts	A	*Omri constructed a beautiful tepee for the Indian.*
respect for others	A	*Omri valued the Indian as a real person with real feelings.*
creativity	A	*Omri solved many problems, such as how to feed and provide shelter for the Indian.*
responsibility	A	*Omri took excellent care of Little Bear.*
attentiveness in school	C	*Omri spent too much time thinking about Little Bear.*

For primary-grade children, descriptors such as "good," "satisfactory," and "needs to improve" may be more appropriate than letter grades.

Example 4.5

- **Title:** *Nate the Great*
- **Author:** Marjorie Weinman Sharmat
- **Grade Level:** K–2
- **Summary:** Nate the Great is a detective whose job is to find a missing picture.

Literary Report Card

Gumshoe Elementary School		
Student: Nate		
G—Good S—Satisfactory N—Needs to Improve		
Area	Grade	Comments
believes in himself	G	*is sure that he can find Annie's lost picture*
can be counted on	G	*leaves a note for his mother when he leaves the house, takes his job very seriously*
is smart	G	*makes plan for finding picture, figures that the only place Fang could bury something is in the backyard, knows red and yellow make orange, figures out where the picture is*
is patient	S	*digs for two hours in the backyard but is in a hurry to leave Rosamond's house and gets mad when Harry paints him*

Example 4.6 _____

- **Title:** *The Tale of Peter Rabbit*
- **Author:** Beatrix Potter
- **Grade Level:** K–2
- **Summary:** Peter Rabbit disobeys his mother and goes to Mr. McGregor's garden. There he is chased by Mr. McGregor and barely escapes.

Literary Report Card

O'Hare Private School

Student: Peter

G—Good   S—Satisfactory   N—Needs to Improve

Areas	Grade	Comments
obedience	N	He went to Mr. McGregor's garden even though his mother told him not to.
bravery	N	He cried a lot when he got caught in a net and when he couldn't find his way out of the garden.
sports	G	He ran fast, jumped into a bucket and out of a window, and wiggled under a fence.

Any grade should be accepted as long as the child is able to provide a reason for the grade. In Example 4.6, some students may give Peter Rabbit an "S" or a "G" in bravery rather than an "N," stating that he was brave to go into McGregor's garden. It is important that the teacher not have correct answers in mind. Rather, he or she must look for reasonable, thoughtful responses and examine students' abilities to substantiate their claims.

It is important that all graded areas be stated in the positive form. It makes no sense to award a character an "A" in impatience, for example, or a "D" in dishonesty.

PLOT ORGANIZERS

Plot organizers provide a visual display of the events that occur in a story. They are useful for helping students summarize a plot and understand its organization, and they also can serve as a model for students' original work (see Chapter Five).

Two plot patterns that may be found in young children's books are the circular and the cumulative patterns. These can be depicted as shown in Examples 4.7 and 4.8.

Example 4.7

- **Title:**   *If You Give a Mouse a Cookie*
- **Author:**   Laura Joffe Numeroff
- **Grade Level:**   K–2
- **Summary:**   A young boy describes the cycle of events that could take place if you give a mouse a cookie.

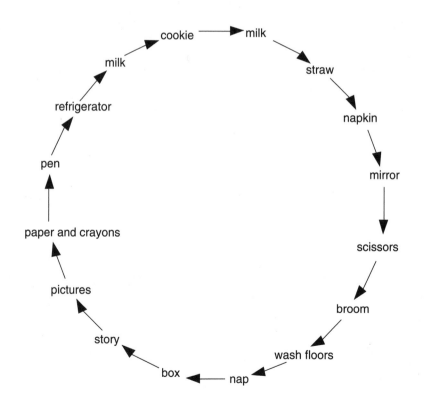

Example 4.8

- **Title:** *This Is the House Where Jack Lives*
- **Author:** Joan Heilbroner
- **Grade Level:** K–2
- **Summary:** This cumulative story tells the consequences of the flooding caused by the overflowing bathtub in which Jack plays.

											Jack
										water	water
									lady	lady	lady
								cook	cook	cook	cook
							cat	cat	cat	cat	cat
						girl	girl	girl	girl	girl	girl
					mop	mop	mop	mop	mop	mop	mop
				man	man	man	man	man	man	man	man
			pail	pail	pail	pail	pail	pail	pail	pail	pail
		boy	boy	boy	boy	boy	boy	boy	boy	boy	boy
	dog	dog	dog	dog	dog	dog	dog	dog	dog	dog	dog
house	house	house	house	house	house	house	house	house	house	house	house

Some cumulative stories, such as *The Napping House*, by Audrey Wood, build to a point and then recede, first adding elements one at a time and then eliminating those elements one at a time until the story ends. This kind of plot structure could be displayed in a stair-step pattern that first rises and then falls. Stair-step organizers also may be used for countdown books such as *Five Little Ducks*, by Ian Beck, and *Five Little Monkeys Jumping on the Bed*, by Eileen Christelow. The stairs are positioned in descending order from left to right.

A plot profile (Johnson & Louis, 1987; see also DeGroff & Galda, 1992) is a more complex type of plot organizer. Students identify the main events in a story and then rate the events along some scale, such as excitement or impact on the character. Events are numbered, and these numbers are placed along a horizontal axis, as in Example 4.9. The rating for each event is plotted along the vertical axis. Lines are drawn between each point, thus creating a line graph. Johnson and Louis suggest that when students rate events in terms of their excitement, they use the following scale: "calm," "very interesting," "exciting," or "WOW!"

Example 4.9 _____

- ■ **Title:** *Number the Stars*
- ■ **Author:** Lois Lowry
- ■ **Summary:** This is the story of one family's efforts to help save Danish Jews from the Nazis.

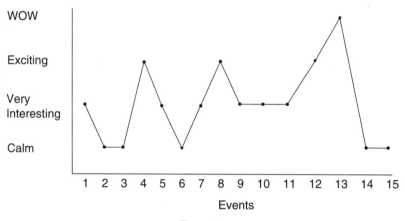

Events

1. Running home from school, Ellen, Annemarie, and Kirsti are stopped by German soldiers.

2. Peter visits after curfew and tells the family that Germans are ordering stores run by Jews closed.

3. Ellen comes to stay with the Johansens when her parents flee.

4. The soldiers search the Johansen apartment for the Rosen family. They challenge Ellen because of her dark hair.

5. Mrs. Johansen, Annemarie, Ellen, and Kirsti travel to Uncle Henrik's.

6. The girls play at Uncle Henrik's.

7. "Aunt Bertie's" loved ones gather around her casket.

8. The soldiers interrupt the gathering.

9. Peter organizes the Jews to head to the boat.

10. Mrs. Johansen leaves with the Rosens.

11. Annemarie sees her mother on the ground and helps her to the house.

12. Annemarie races through the woods to deliver the envelope to Henrik.

13. Annemarie is stopped and questioned by soldiers. They discover the package.

14. Uncle Henrik explains the Resistance and the handkerchief to Annemarie.

15. The war ends. Annemarie learns the truth about Lise's death.

An alternative to a line graph is a cut-and-paste grid. Students write each event from the story on a separate piece of paper. These may be illustrated. Students then paste these sheets higher or lower on a large butcher paper grid, depending upon the ratings they give. The key events and ratings shown in the line graph in Example 4.9 are depicted in the cut-and-paste format in Example 4.10.

Children can work individually or they can collaborate in small groups on plot profiles, coming to consensus on story events and ratings. If other individuals or groups of students are reading the same book, plot profiles can be compared. Teachers should expect differences between individual or group selections of key events and ratings.

Example 4.10 _____

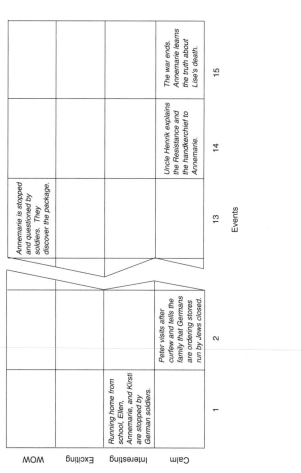

WORLD WHEELS

A world wheel may be used to help students organize information from books that present variations on experiences that people around the world share. For instance, in *This Is the Way We Go to School*, Edith Baer introduces readers to children traveling to their respective schools in more than twenty locations throughout the world. Children are seen riding their bikes to school in China, taking the elevated rail transit in Chicago, Illinois, and traveling by train in Kenya. In *Bread Bread Bread*, by Ann Morris, readers are introduced to many different kinds of bread that are enjoyed in different ways around the world. In *This Is My House*, by Arthur Dorros, readers learn about the similarities and differences among homes around the world, and in *Talking Walls*, by Margy Burns Knight, children are exposed to landmark walls around the world, including the Great Wall of China, the ancient walls of the Lascaux cave in France, the Wailing Wall in Jerusalem, the carved walls in Mahabalipuram, India, and the Berlin Wall.

World wheels help readers summarize the information in these books. In the examples below, students have included in their world wheel only some of the information included in the books. Students may choose information that they find most interesting, information related to countries they have studied, information related to countries represented in the classroom, or, in the case of the example that follows, information about hopscotch activities they would like to try. Of course, if the students wish to include all information offered by the text, they should not be discouraged—with some books the wheel will have many spokes!

Example 4.11

- **Title:** *Hopscotch Around the World*
- **Author:** May D. Lankford
- **Grade Level:** 2–6
- **Summary:** The reader learns that hopscotch is an ancient game that is played in a variety of forms around the world. A brief narrative about each of nineteen regions and detailed directions for nineteen versions of the game are provided.

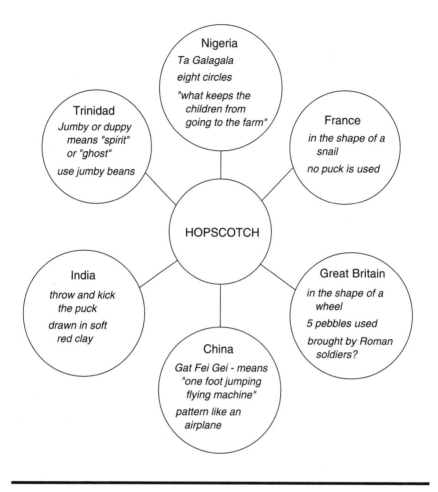

Nigeria
Ta Galagala
eight circles
"what keeps the children from going to the farm"

Trinidad
Jumby or duppy means "spirit" or "ghost"
use jumby beans

France
in the shape of a snail
no puck is used

HOPSCOTCH

India
throw and kick the puck
drawn in soft red clay

China
Gat Fei Gei - means "one foot jumping flying machine"
pattern like an airplane

Great Britain
in the shape of a wheel
5 pebbles used
brought by Roman soldiers?

Example 4.12

- **Title:** *Welcoming Babies*
- **Author:** Margy Burns Knight
- **Grade Level:** K–3
- **Summary:** "Every day, everywhere, babies are born. We have many ways to show them we are glad they came into the world." So begins this book that introduces readers to the many ways people of different cultures welcome newborns into the world.

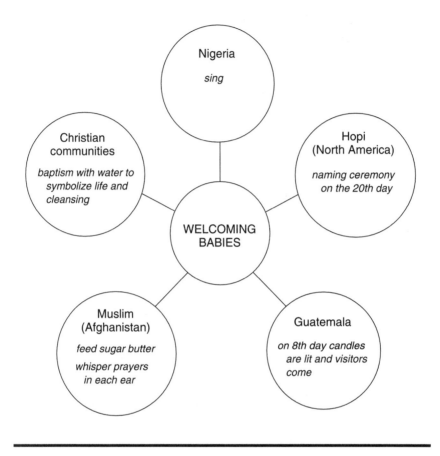

World wheels provide a vehicle for organizing information that students find in books that expose them to the diversity in the world, and at the same time help them understand what is common in the human experience. The strategy can serve as a stimulus for students' exploration of their own backgrounds and pique their interest in learning about the cultural heritage of others. Students could be encouraged to include an additional spoke in which they record their own personal experience. In Example 4.11 they could include "How I play hopscotch"; in Example 4.12 they could include "How I was welcomed into the world." Discussions with family would enrich this activity.

VENN DIAGRAMS

Venn diagrams offer a means for students to compare and contrast story elements (such as characters) in a book or to compare and contrast two or more books. Venn diagrams provide graphic representations of common and contrasting features. The teacher may introduce Venn diagrams by drawing two overlapping circles on the chalkboard. The circles represent the different elements or different books. Where the circles overlap, attributes that two elements have in common or content shared by two books is recorded. In the non-overlapping portions of the circles, attributes that are unique to each element or book are recorded. Example 4.13 displays a Venn diagram comparing and contrasting fruit bats and birds from the book *Stellaluna.*

Example 4.13 _____

- **Title:** *Stellaluna*
- **Author:** Janell Cannon
- **Grade Level:** K–3
- **Summary:** A fruit bat is cared for by a family of birds after falling from its mother's grasp while fleeing an owl. The bat and birds find that even though they are different, they are alike.

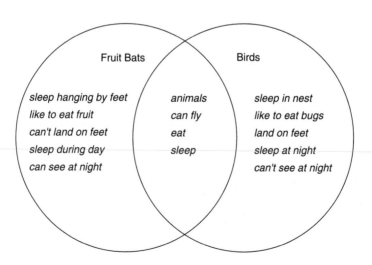

Comparisons can be made across books. For instance, the perspectives and actions of Johnny in *Johnny Tremain*, by Esther Forbes, can be compared and contrasted with those of Tim in *My Brother Sam Is Dead*, by James Lincoln Collier and Christopher Collier. Each of these characters is a boy who lives during the time of the American Revolution. Example 4.14 shows a Venn diagram for *Adam of the Road*, by Elizabeth Janet Gray, and *The Door in the Wall*, by Marguerite de Angeli. Each of these books details the experiences of a boy growing up during the Middle Ages.

Example 4.14

- **Titles:**   *Adam of the Road* (Elizabeth Janet Gray)
                The Door in the Wall (Marguerite de Angeli)
- **Grade Level:** 5–8

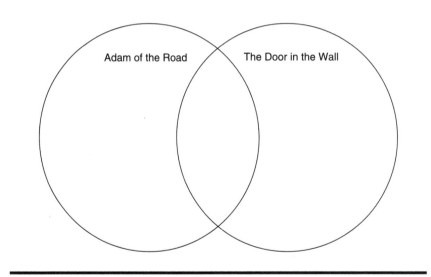

An interesting variation on this activity is to have students use Venn diagrams to compare themselves to a character. In Example 4.15, students can compare their lifestyles to that of a young boy whose people had a Stone Age way of life. In Example 4.16, students can compare modern American weddings to those of medieval times in Europe.

Example 4.15 _____

- **Title:**   *Lobo of the Tasaday*

- **Author:**   John Nance

- **Grade Level:**   2–5

- **Summary:**   Lobo is a young member of the Tasaday, a group of people who live in a rain forest on an island in the southern Philippines. The author tells the true story of their Stone Age lifestyle and their discovery by the modern world in 1971.

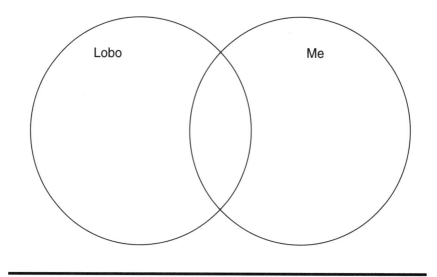

Example 4.16 _____

- **Title:**   *Merry Ever After: The Story of Two Medieval Weddings*

- **Author:**   Joe Lasker

- **Grade Level:**   3–6

- **Summary:**   The author provides the students with information on weddings from medieval times. Specifically, he compares a noble wedding with a peasant wedding.

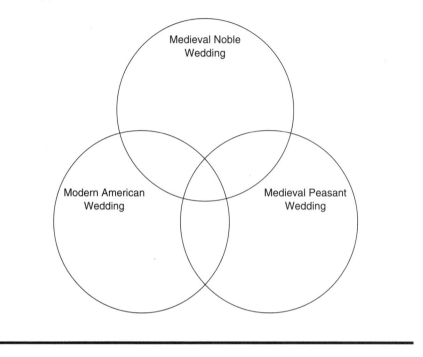

BOOK CHARTS

Book charts provide a structure for making comparisons among books, thus moving the students beyond "local reading" (Wolf in Hartman & Hartman, 1993)—a narrow focus on individual works of literature with little or no effort to make connections across texts. Through the use of book charts, students can discover patterns in literature, identify conventions in certain genres of literature, and come to recognize the universality of specific themes. Their roles as readers are expanded beyond "the boundaries of a single text" (Hartman & Hartman, p. 202). Students can compare and contrast characters' experiences and their responses to those experiences, analyze similarities and differences in plots, and examine authors' strategies for developing common themes.

If students have read or listened to *In the Year of the Boar and Jackie Robinson* by Bette Lord, *Dragonwings* by Laurence Yep, and *Journey to America* by Sonia Levitin, then a book chart that focuses on the theme "immigrants" may be useful for recording information and making comparisons. Several categories may be listed on a chart. In the immigrant example, categories might include "book," "author," "character," "native country," "positive experiences," and "negative experiences." Upon the completion of each book, information is written in the chart. Book charts may be developed by individual students or small groups, or large class charts may be generated. Class charts may be written on butcher paper and pinned to a bulletin board to remain in view for weeks or even months, depending upon the number of books included on the chart. Completed book charts will prove to be useful guides for students as they write analytical papers or their own stories on the same theme.

Example 4.17

- **Grade Level:** 3–6
- **Theme:** Lessons

Book Chart

Title	Author	Character	Lesson
The War with Grandpa	*Robert K. Smith*	*Peter*	*War isn't fun. War doesn't solve problems.*
The Hundred Dresses	*Eleanor Estes*	*Maddie*	*Don't just stand by when others are doing cruel things.*
Eyes of the Dragon	*Margaret Leaf*	*The magistrate*	*It is important to keep your word.*

The Cay by Theodore Taylor, *Call of the Wild* by Jack London, and *The Pinballs* by Betsy Byars, appropriate for grades 6 and up, could be used on a chart focusing on "obstacles," since the main characters in each of these books must overcome obstacles such as prejudice, physical disabilities, unforeseen circumstances, and abusive relationships in order to survive (psychologically or physically). A "survival" theme could be the focus of a book chart that includes *The Sign of the Beaver* by Elizabeth George Speare, *Island of the Blue Dolphins* by Scott O'Dell, *Hatchet* by Gary Paulsen, and *Julie of the Wolves* by Jean Craighead George. In each of these books, the protagonist is stranded alone somewhere and must find strength from within to survive the elements. Categories on the book chart might include author, title, reason the protagonist is alone, challenges faced, and outcome.

Book charts are also appropriate for primary-grade students. Three books that have a character who makes wishes are *Sylvester and the Magic Pebble* by William Steig, *The Magic Fish* by Freya Littledale, and *The Three Wishes* by M. Jean Craig. Students may be asked to identify the title of the book, the author, and the wishes. The consequences of the wishes could be discussed and students could be asked to share wishes they themselves might make. This example and the one depicted below may be used with kindergarteners or even preschool children. With younger children, the teacher will play a greater role in facilitating discussions and recording information.

Example 4.18

- **Grade Level:**   Primary
- **Theme:**   Believing

Book Chart

Title	Author	Who Believes	What He/She Believes
The Carrot Seed	*Ruth Krauss*	*little boy*	*his carrot seed will grow*
Mike Mulligan and His Steam Shovel	*Virginia Lee Burton*	*Mike Mulligan*	*his steam shovel will be able to dig as much in one day as 100 men can do in one week*
The Little Engine That Could	*Watty Piper*	*little engine*	*it can get up the hill*
Katy and the Big Snow	*Virginia Lee Burton*	*tractor*	*she can plow the snow*

Western (1980) describes a book chart in which students compare the characters, setting, problem, and ending of three versions of *Jack and the Beanstalk* and analyze their similarities and differences. A framework for this type of book chart using three versions of the Cinderella story is provided in Example 4.19.

Example 4.19

- **Titles:** *Yeh-Shen: A Cinderella Story from China* (Ai-Ling Louie)

  Moss Gown (William H. Hooks)

  The Egyptian Cinderella (Shirley Climo)

- **Grade Level:** 2–5

Book Chart

Version

	Yeh-Shen	Moss Gown	The Egyptian Cinderella	Similarities	Differences	Conclusions
Characters						
Setting						
Problem						
Ending						

TABLE TALK

Another activity that encourages students to reflect on characters and search for links among several books is table talk, adapted from Ragle (1994). After reading two or more books, students are asked to organize a dinner party for several guests—characters they select from the books. Students determine the seating arrangement and provide the rationale for their choices. In addition, students identify possible topics of conversation that could occur between guests seated near one another. What, for instance, might Jonas of *The Giver* (Lowry, 1993) talk about with Meg of *A Wrinkle in Time* (L'Engle, 1962)? If students have developed character maps or literature maps for these books, this strategy will be easier, since students can draw on notes developed through their previous efforts.

The students begin—as a large group, small group, or individually—by drawing a square in the center of a page. This is the table at which the guests will be seated. Then students select characters whom they will seat at the table. They decide who will be placed next to whom, place the names in position around the table, and state why each pair of characters is together. Although Example 4.20 shows the main character from each of the books, students may select any character they wish to invite to dinner— the protagonist, the antagonist, a supporting character, or a minor character.

Once students have indicated their reasons for placing certain characters together, they then further elaborate on the chart by identifying possible topics of conversation that might occur between each pair of characters. A natural extension of the diagram is to have students provide specific examples of dialogue between the characters, using the characters' voices. Ultimately, this map could be used as a springboard for writing a play or a narrative piece.

Students might enjoy having the opportunity to include themselves in the dinner party. Again, they should provide the rationale for their placement between characters at the table and indicate topics that they would discuss with each character seated next to them during the meal.

This strategy facilitates students' understanding of characters and their view of common issues, ideas, or experiences across books. They may come to appreciate different points of view on the same issue, different responses to similiar experiences, and the universality of some human experiences.

Example 4.20

- **Books:** *A Gathering of Days* (Joan Blos)

    The Slave Dancer (Paula Fox)

    Cezanne Pinto (Mary Stolz)

    Amos Fortune, Free Man (Elizabeth Yates)
- **Grade Level:** 5–8

Topics of Conversation

horrors of slave trade

experiences at sea

Topics of Conversation

cruelty of slavery

what Africa was like

different experiences as slaves

different ways of becoming free

experiences as free men

why?

both experienced
crossing the ocean
on a slave ship

Amos Fortune

why?

both were slaves
who ultimately
became free

Jessie

Cezanne Pinto

why?

both witnessed some
aspects of slavery and
tried to help

Catherine Hall

why?

lived during same period
of time

he was a runaway
slave; she helped one

Topics of Conversation

respective experiences
of slavery

what can be done to
help

Topics of Conversation

life as a runaway

life as a slave

Underground Railroad

CONCLUSION

Postreading activities are useful for enhancing students' comprehension of, personal response to, and appreciation for literature. Polar opposites, literary report cards, and table talk provide interesting and motivating formats for thinking about and analyzing characters. Venn diagrams, world wheels, book charts, and plot organizers offer means for summarizing, organizing, and integrating information. Each of these seven types of postreading activities provides an opportunity for students to listen, speak, read, and write and encourages critical thinking. Most are open-ended and allow students to bring their individuality to the activity. Hopefully, teachers will take the time to engage students in postreading activities such as these that encourage students to continue to think about characters, issues, and events in and across books after they have read them.

REFERENCES

Baer, E. (1990). *This is the way we go to school.* New York: Scholastic.

Banks, L. (1982). *The Indian in the cupboard.* New York: Avon.

Beck, I. (1992). *Five little ducks.* New York: The Trumpet Club.

Blos, J. (1979). *A gathering of days: A New England girl's journal 1930–1832.* New York: Aladdin.

Burton, V. L. (1943). *Katy and the big snow.* Boston: Houghton.

Burton, V. L. (1967). *Mike Mulligan and his steam shovel.* Boston: Houghton Mifflin.

Byars, B. (1977). *The pinballs.* New York: Harper & Row.

Cannon, J. (1993). *Stellaluna.* San Diego, CA: Harcourt Brace.

Christelow, E. (1989). *Five little monkeys jumping on the bed.* New York: Clarion.

Climo, S. (1989). *The Egyptian Cinderella.* New York: Thomas Y. Crowell.

Collier, J. L. & Collier, C. (1974). *My brother Sam is dead.* New York: Four Winds.

Craig, M. J. (1968). *The three wishes.* New York: Scholastic.

de Angeli, M. (1949). *The door in the wall.* New York: Scholastic.

DeGroff, L., & Galda, L. (1992) Responding to literature: Activities for exploring books. In B. Cullinan (Ed.), *Invitation to read: More children's literature in the reading program.* Newark, DE: International Reading Association.

Dorros, A. (1992). *This is my house.* New York: Scholastic.

Estes, E. (1974). *The hundred dresses.* San Diego: Harcourt Brace Jovanovich.

Forbes, E. (1971). *Johnny Tremain.* New York: Dell.

Fox, P. (1973). *The slave dancer.* New York: Dell.

Frost, R. (1959). *You come too.* New York: Holt, Rinehart, & Winston.

George, J. C. (1972). *Julie of the wolves.* New York: Harper & Row.

Gray, E. J. (1942). *Adam of the road.* New York: Puffin.

Hartman, D. K. & Hartman, J. A. (1993). Reading across texts: Expanding the role of the reader. *The Reading Teacher, 47,* 202–211.

Heilbroner, J. (1962). *This is the house where Jack lives.* New York: Harper & Row.

Hooks, W. (1987). *Moss gown.* New York: Clarion Books.

Johnson, T. & Louis, D. (1987). *Literacy through literature.* Portsmouth, NH: Heinemann.

Konigsburg, E. L. (1974). *From the mixed-up files of Mrs. Basil E. Frankweiler*. New York: Dell.

Knight, M. B. (1992). *Talking walls*. Gardiner, ME: Tilbury House.

Knight, M. B. (1994). *Welcoming babies*. Gardiner, ME: Tilbury House.

Krauss, R. (1945). *The carrot seed*. New York: Harper and Brothers.

Lankford, M. (1992). *Hopscotch around the world*. New York: Morrow Junior Books.

Lasker, J. (1976). *Merry ever after: The story of two medieval weddings*. New York: Viking.

Leaf, M. (1967). *The story of Ferdinand*. New York: Scholastic.

Leaf, M. (1987). *Eyes of the dragon*. New York: Lothrop, Lee & Shepard.

L'Engle, M. (1962). *A wrinkle in time*. New York: Farrar, Straus and Giroux.

Levitin, S. (1971). *Journey to America*. New York: Atheneum.

Littledale, F. (1986). *The magic fish*. New York: Scholastic.

London, J. (1974). *Call of the wild*. New York: Simon & Schuster.

Lord, B. (1984). *In the year of the boar and Jackie Robinson*. New York: Harper Junior Books.

Louie, A. L. (1982). *Yeh-Shen: A Cinderella story from China*. New York: Philomel.

Lowry, L. (1989). *Number the stars*. New York: Dell.

Lowry, L. (1993). *The giver*. Boston: Houghton Mifflin.

Morris, A. (1989). *Bread bread bread*. New York: Mulberry.

Nance, J. (1982). *Lobo of the Tasaday*. New York: Pantheon.

Numeroff, L. J. (1985). *If you give a mouse a cookie*. New York: Harper & Row.

O'Dell, S. (1960). *Island of the blue dolphins*. Boston: Houghton Mifflin.

Paulsen, G. (1987). *Hatchet*. New York: The Trumpet Club.

Piper, W. (1985). *The little engine that could*. New York: Scholastic.

Potter, B. (1989). *The tale of Peter Rabbit*. London: Penguin.

Ragle, M. (1994). Guess who's coming to dinner? *Newsletter of the English Council of Orange County* (Summer).

Sharmat, M. (1977). *Nate the great*. New York: Dell.

Smith, R. (1984). *The war with Grandpa*. New York: Delacorte.

Speare, E. G. (1983). *The sign of the beaver*. Boston: Houghton Mifflin.

Steig, W. (1969). *Sylvester and the magic pebble*. New York: Simon & Schuster.

Stolz, M. (1994). *Cezanne Pinto*. New York: Alfred A. Knopf.

Taylor, T. (1970). *The cay*. New York: Avon.

Western, L. (1980). A comparative study of literature through folk tale variants. *Language Arts, 57*, 395–402.

Wood, A. (1984). *The napping house*. San Diego, CA: Harcourt Brace Jovanovich.

Yates, E. (1950). *Amos Fortune, Free Man*. New York: Dutton.

Yep, L. (1975). *Dragonwings*. New York: Harper Junior Books.

C H A P T E R   F I V E

Bookmaking

Bookmaking

Purposes

- To motivate children to read and write
- To stimulate creativity
- To provide a means for sharing students' writing
- To promote problem solving and decision making
- To promote comprehension and language development

Activities

- Pop-up books
- Accordion books
- Fold-up books
- Upside-down books
- Retelling picture books

Publishing student books in the classroom is a natural extension of reading books and a wonderful way to integrate the language arts. Educators have long recognized the value of children's participation in literary experiences. What activity involves children more intensely in the literary experience than having them write, construct, and share their own books in response to a selection just read? Bookmaking moves children away from the notion of writing as an exercise to demonstrate skills toward an understanding of writing and reading as exciting, personally meaningful, communicative activities. Indeed, students gain a greater sense of audience (Bromley, 1988; Holdaway, 1979), and they are more likely to make spontaneous revisions in their writing (DeFord, 1984) when they engage in bookmaking. Furthermore, unlike traditional writing activities, bookmaking encourages students to reread their own writing and that of their classmates often.

When developing books as a response to literature, children may summarize the original author's work or borrow the author's literary structure to create a new work. Summarization requires students to identify important events or concepts for inclusion in their books and to make decisions about organizing information over a series of pages. Research has demonstrated that children's reconstruction of a story results in increased comprehension (Brown, 1975) and enhances their concept of story structure and their oral language (Koskinen, Gambrell, Kapinus, & Heathington, 1988; Morrow, 1985).

An alternative to summarization is patterned writing. In patterned writing the author's literary structure, or pattern, provides a scaffold for writing an original work (Peregoy & Boyle, 1990). Predictable books serve as the best models for patterned writing. A book that follows a repetitious pattern, such as *Over in the Meadow*, retold by John Langstaff, is ideal. In this book, the author describes ten meadow animals. The rhythm and use of rhyme remain the same throughout the story. The students may change the setting and the animals in the story to create their own books, while maintaining the author's patterns. For example, they may write *Over in the Forest*, or *Over in the Desert*. This will be especially interesting if the students are studying habitats in science. Another option is to have students continue with the author's setting and add an eleventh meadow animal, a twelfth, and so on.

The repetition in *The Little Red Hen*, by Vera Southgate, is also easily modeled. Students select an activity other than the planting of seeds, such as the baking of cupcakes, and identify and list the steps required in performing that activity. Then they use the language of *The Little Red Hen*, substituting the cupcake activity. In addition, the students might provide different characters, such as relatives or friends. Each responds with "Not I," following the pattern established by the author.

The House That Jack Built, by David Cutts, and *I Know an Old Lady*, by Rose Bonne, both of which follow cumulative patterns, are excellent choices for patterned writing, as are books such as *Chicken Soup with Rice*, by Maurice Sendak, and *The Very Hungry Caterpillar*, by Eric Carle, which follow sequence patterns.

Another method for modeling the language of an author is copy change, or creative imitation (Leyson,1989). Copy change does not require the use of predictable books. The teacher may use a selection from any book he or she believes models effective language. Students are asked to rewrite the passage, making specified changes. The rewriting possibilities are endless and may include the following:

1. Changing the setting.
2. Changing the main character from a female to a male.
3. Changing verbs from present tense to past tense.
4. Changing from a third-person voice to a first-person voice.
5. Changing all adjectives.

Student versions of the passage may be bound together in a class-room book and displayed.

The notion of displaying books is an important one. Student books should not be created and then set aside. Rather, they should be placed in a classroom library or in any location where they are visible and accessible. Classroom books are intended to be handled and read over and over again. Sharing need not be restricted to the immediate classroom. Students may read their books to children in other classrooms or take one home overnight and share it with family members.

Many student-created books contain a "reader-response" page. This page typically is placed at the end of the book and invites written comments from readers, including other students, classroom guests, the principal, parents, and siblings. What a wonderful opportunity for authors to experience an audience and receive feedback!

In the remainder of this chapter, we provide directions for con-structing *pop-up books, accordion books, fold-up books, upside-down books*, and *retelling picture books*. Each of these book types may be used as a vehicle for summarizing a work of literature or modeling the language and ideas in a selection. Each may be developed and constructed by individuals or groups.

The purposes of engaging children in bookmaking activities are as follows:

- To motivate children to read and write.
- To stimulate creativity.
- To provide a means for sharing.
- To promote problem solving and decision making.
- To promote comprehension and language development.

POP-UP BOOKS

Pop-up books are fun and easy to construct. Children love the three-dimensional nature of these books, and parents are always impressed with their child's product. To make each page of the book, follow these simple directions:

1. Fold a piece of paper in half. Construction paper provides the best thickness and support for the pop-up pictures, but ditto paper will do. Make two cuts of equal length about one inch apart into the creased edge of the paper.

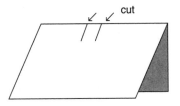

2. Open the paper so the two halves form a right angle. Pull the cut section through and fold it inward.

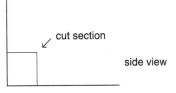

3. Paste a picture onto the cut section as shown.

You will probably want to have your students draw background pictures prior to pasting the pop-ups onto the page. The narrative also should be written on the paper prior to pasting and is typically on the bottom half of the paper.

Several pop-up figures may be placed on one page. Their size can vary by making shorter or longer cuts and by making the cuts closer together or farther apart. Each page should be constructed separately.

4. Fold each paper back in half, stack the pages in order, and glue.

ACCORDION BOOKS

Accordion books are a wonderful activity for cooperative learning groups and provide an excellent opportunity for problem solving. First, the students must divide a reading selection into meaningful sections. The number of sections will depend partly on the age of the students. Very young students, for example, may identify only the beginning, middle, and end of a selection. Once the group determines the sections, each student illustrates and writes a brief narrative for one of the sections on a 9-by-12-inch piece of tagboard. The boards are then lined up end to end and taped or tied together in sequence. Books may stand freely on counters accordion-style or be folded for storage.

To ensure a cohesive product, group members should thoroughly discuss and agree upon narration and illustrations prior to making individual assignments. If students do not discuss details, they run the risk of having a final product that lacks continuity and is clumsy. For example, one page may be written in the present tense and the next in the past tense, or the protagonist may be blond on one page and brunette on the next.

It is always interesting to have groups share their completed books. Students will notice that each group chose to summarize and illustrate the selection differently. Groups may vary in the events they chose to depict and in their illustrations.

Younger children may need to be guided through the summarization of the selection and the assignment of individual sections.

FOLD-UP BOOKS

Students can create a book that opens like a traditional book by folding and cutting a single sheet of paper. The size of the book will depend upon the size of the paper used. Some students will enjoy making Big Books (Holdaway, 1979) using butcher paper, and others will prefer to make miniatures using an 8½-by-11-inch piece of paper. Directions must be followed carefully.

1. Fold a rectangular piece of paper into eighths as shown, pressing firmly on the creases. Open the paper, then refold the opposite direction on the same folds, again creasing firmly.

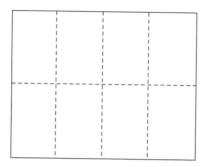

2. Fold the paper in half and cut on the center line as shown.

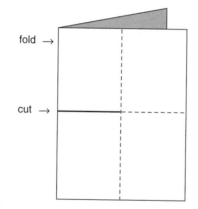

3. Open the paper. Lift points *a* and *c*, pulling them upwards and away from each other so that points *b* and *d* come together. This will be difficult if folds are not well-creased.

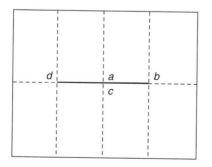

Your paper should look like this from the top:

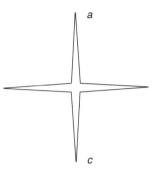

4. Bring all flaps together to form the book. Crease all folds.

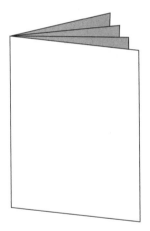

5. Students may then summarize the story and illustrate each page.

UPSIDE-DOWN BOOKS

This type of book is most useful when contrasting ideas are discussed or suggested by a piece of literature. One idea may be written on one side of a piece of paper, and the contrasting idea may be written upside down on the reverse side. For example, students may write about both a horrible, terrible day and a wonderful, delightful day after reading the story *Alexander and the Terrible, Horrible, No Good, Very Bad Day*, by Judith Viorst. Use the following format:

1. Each student completes a prompt such as "It was a horrible, terrible, no good, very bad day when . . . ." on a piece of paper and illustrates it.

2. Upside down and on the reverse side of the paper, each student completes and illustrates a second prompt such as "It was a wonderful, delightful, marvelous, fantastic day when . . . ." (Students may complete the second picture and narration on a separate piece of paper. Papers may subsequently be pasted on a sheet of construction paper, one on the front and one upside down on the back.)

3. All student papers are collected and stacked together, the same side up. In other words, all the "horrible day" sentences and illustrations are facing up, and all the "wonderful day" sentences and illustrations are facing down (and are upside down). An appropriate title page should be put on the front and the back. Bind the pages with staples, ribbons, brads, or whatever is available. When the book is read in one direction, it is the story of very bad days. When the book is turned over and upside down, it is the story of wonderful days.

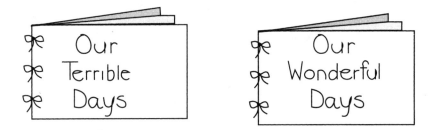

Information recorded in a contrast chart can provide ideas for an upside-down book. For example, the advantages and disadvantages of being two inches tall were listed in a contrast chart for *Stuart Little*, by E. B. White, in Chapter Two of this book. Students may create an upside-down book based on this chart with one side of the paper illustrating "A good thing about being two inches tall is . . . ." and the reverse side of the paper illustrating "A bad thing about being two inches tall is . . . ."

RETELLING PICTURE BOOKS

Retelling picture books allow students to retell stories with the help of attached characters that can be moved on and off the pages of a book. First, settings are identified and illustrations are drawn, painted, or cut and pasted onto pieces of paper that become the pages of the book. A title page is created that includes a pocket in which characters may be stored. The pages are then bound together by any means.

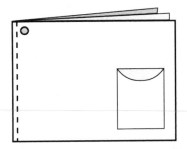

Next, characters are drawn onto tagboard and cut out. A hole is punched in each character, and a ribbon is tied through the hole. The other end of the ribbon is tied through a hole punched in the upper left-hand corner of the book. The ribbons must be long enough so that the students can move the characters freely. Three feet is a good length.

Students may then move the characters onto each page of the book as they retell the story.

One student teacher constructed a retelling picture book with a class of kindergarteners. She had each of her students make the following illustrations for *Goldilocks and the Three Bears*, by Lorinda Bryan Cauley, on 12-by-18-inch pieces of construction paper:

Page 1: the bears' house in the middle of a forest

Page 2: three bowls of porridge with the words "Papa," "Mama," and "Baby" written on them

Page 3: three chairs and a stairway

Page 4: three beds

After a title page was created and the pages were bound together, each student drew a picture of Goldilocks on tagboard and cut it out. Each also drew the three bears, cut them out, and pasted them together side by side so they could be moved about as a single entity. Goldilocks and the bears were then connected by ribbons to a corner of the book as just described.

When the children retold the story, they removed the characters from the pocket on the title page, opened the first page of the book, and moved the appropriate characters onto the page. On page 1, the Bears were moved from the house into the forest to go for a walk. Goldilocks was moved onto the page to discover the bears' open house. On page 2, Goldilocks was moved from bowl to bowl before finding Baby Bear's porridge just right to eat. The students continued retelling the story while moving the characters from page to page.

A retelling picture book provides students with a structure for retelling a story, and the scenes serve as reminders for each part of the story. Retelling picture books are very motivational and serve as wonderful vehicles for language development. Furthermore, this activity is adaptable to many grade levels. Older children may make books for younger children or may develop a retelling picture book for a section of a novel they are reading.

CONCLUSION

Constructing their own books in response to literature is a highly motivational activity that promotes children's comprehension and language development. In addition, it reinforces a view of reading and writing as acts of communication. It is one of the most meaningful literacy activities in which students of any age can engage, and at the same time it can be supportive of other areas of the curriculum.

REFERENCES

Bonne, R. (1985). *I know an old lady.* New York: Scholastic.

Bromley, K. (1988). *Language arts: Exploring connections.* Boston: Allyn and Bacon.

Brown, A. (1975). Recognition, reconstruction, and recall of narrative sequences of preoperational children. *Child Development, 46,* 155–156.

Carle, E. (1987). *The very hungry caterpillar.* New York: Scholastic.

Cauley, L. B. (1981). *Goldilocks and the three bears.* New York: Putnam.

Cutts, D. (1979). *The house that Jack built.* Mahwah, NJ: Troll Associates.

DeFord, D. (1984). Classroom context for literacy learning. In T. Raphael (Ed.), *The context of school-based literacy* (pp. 163–180). New York: Random House.

Holdaway, D. (1979). *The foundations of literacy.* Exerter, NH: Heinemann.

Koskinen, P., Gambrell, L., Kapinus, B., & Heathington, B. (1988). Retelling: A strategy for enhancing students' reading comprehension. *The Reading Teacher, 41,* 892–896.

Langstaff, J. (1973). *Over in the meadow.* New York: Harcourt Brace Jovanovich.

Leyson, E. (1989). Authors teach literacy: Modeling, imitating, creating. In *From literacy to literature: Reading and writing for the language-minority student* (pp.163–198). Los Angeles: Center for Academic Interinstitutional Programs, University of California.

Morrow, L. M. (1985). Retelling stories: A strategy for improving young children's comprehension, concept of story structure, and oral language complexity. *The Elementary School Journal, 85* (5), 647–661.

Peregoy, S. & Boyle, O. (1990). Reading and writing scaffolds: Supporting literacy for second language learners. *Educational Issues of Language Minority Students, 6,* 55–67.

Sendak, M. (1986). *Chicken soup with rice.* New York: Scholastic.

Southgate, V. (1966). *The little red hen.* Loughborough, England: Wills & Hepworth.

Viorst, J. (1976). *Alexander and the terrible, horrible, no good, very bad day.* New York: Macmillan.

White, E. B. (1973). *Stuart Little.* New York: Harper & Row.

Afterword

We hope that teachers will find the activities described in this book useful for promoting meaningful interactions with literature and inspiring a love of reading in their students. Before teachers incorporate these activities into their literature programs, however, we would like to issue a few cautions.

First, it is important that teachers know their students and make instructional decisions based upon students' interests and needs. Activities that are appropriate for some individuals may be less valuable for others. For example, some students may have considerable background knowledge on a particular topic and so will need less time devoted to building background knowledge prior to interacting with the selection. Other students may have little background knowledge on the topic and will profit from participation in a number of prereading activities.

Second, teachers should not be surprised if students do not engage in a grand conversation the first time an activity is attempted. Many children have experienced only gentle (or not so gentle!) inquisitions in school settings. They have learned that there is only one correct answer, that the most verbal students will provide it, or that if they wait long enough the teacher will provide it. This is especially true of older students who have had more time to learn these lessons. Given these expectations, it is not likely that all students will respond enthusiastically to the activities at first. Teachers must attempt the activities several times before achieving participation from everyone, while at the same time building trust and new expectations in their students.

Third, these activities should not be used as worksheets that are to be completed independently and collected for a grade. They are intended to arouse curiosity, activate background knowledge, focus attention on themes or language, promote comprehension, encourage reflection on issues or events encountered in books, and help students find literature selections personally meaningful. Few independently completed worksheets achieve these goals. They can be achieved, however, through meaningful interaction among students and with the teacher.

Fourth, literature activities should not be overused. We know one teacher who implemented several prereading activities before every chapter of a novel. We were not surprised when she told us that her students disliked the novel, and lost enthusiasm for the activities. Anything can be overdone. Teachers should exercise reason when using literature activities before, during, and after reading. Sometimes it is most appropriate to use none at all.

112

Finally, teachers should provide students with many opportunities to read and listen to literature in the classroom throughout the day and in many contexts. These opportunities, along with an extensive classroom library, will go a long way toward promoting a love of reading.

APPENDIX A

Resources for Teachers

PROFESSIONAL BOOKS AND DOCUMENTS

Bissex, G. (1980). *Gnys at wrk. A child learns to write and read.* Cambridge, MA: Harvard University Press.

Celebrating the National Reading Initiative. (1989). Sacramento, CA: California State Department of Education.

Cullinan, B. E. (1987). *Children's literature in the reading program.* Newark, DE: International Reading Association.

Cullinan, B. E. (1992). *Invitation to read: More children's literature in the reading program.* Newark, DE: International Reading Association.

Cullinan, B. E. (1993). *Fact and fiction: Literature across the curriculum.* Newark, DE: International Reading Association.

Fields, M., Spangler, K., & Lee, D. (1991). *Let's begin reading right. Developmentally appropriate beginning literacy* (2nd ed.). New York: Macmillan.

From literacy to literature. Reading and writing for the language-minority student. (1989). Los Angeles: Center for Academic Interinstitutional Programs, University of California.

Glazer, J. (1991). *Literature for young children.* New York: Macmillan.

Hancock, J., & Hill, S. (1987). *Literature-based reading programs at work.* Portsmouth, NH: Heinemann.

Heller, M. (1991). *Reading-writing connections. From theory to practice.* New York: Longman.

Hennings, D. G. (1992). *Beyond the read aloud: Learning to read through listening to and reflecting on literature.* Bloomington, IN: Phi Delta Kappa.

Hickman, J., & Cullinan, B. (1989). *Children's literature in the classroom: Weaving Charlotte's web.* Needham Heights, MA: Christopher-Gordon.

Holdaway, D. (1979). *The foundations of literacy.* New York: Ashton Scholastic.

Huck, C., Hepler, S., & Hickman, J. (1993). *Children's literature in the elementary school* (5th ed.). Orlando: Harcourt Brace Jovanovich.

Irvine, J. (1987). *How to make pop-ups.* New York: Beech Tree Books.

Johnson, P. (1990). *A book of one's own.* Portsmouth, NH: Heinemann.

Johnson, P. (1992). *Pop-up paper engineering.* London: The Falmer Press.

Johnson, T., & Louis, D. (1987). *Literacy through literature.* Portsmouth, NH: Heinemann.

Nelms, B. (1988). *Literature in the classroom: Readers, texts, and contexts.* Urbana, IL: National Council of Teachers of English.

Norton, D. (1991). *Through the eyes of a child. An introduction to children's literature* (3rd ed.). New York: Macmillan.

Pappas, C., Keifer, B., & Levstik, L. (1990). *An integrated language perspective in the elementary school.* New York: Longman.

Parsons, L. (1990). *Response journals.* Portsmouth, NH: Heinemann.

Routman, R. (1988). *Transitions: From literature to literacy.* Portsmouth, NH: Heinemann.

Routman, R. (1991). *Innovations: Changing as teachers and learners K–12.* Portsmouth, NH: Heinemann.

Scarffe, B., & Wilson, L. (1988). *You can't make a book in a day: A practical guide to classroom publishing.* Victoria, Australia: Robert Andersen & Associates.

Slaughter, J. P. (1993). *Beyond storybooks: Young children and the shared book experience.* Newark, DE: International Reading Association.

Smith, F. (1983). *Essays into literacy.* Portsmouth, NH: Heinemann.

Smith, F. (1988). *Insult to intelligence.* Portsmouth, NH: Heinemann.

Spangenberg-Urbschat, K., & Pritchard, R. (1994). *Kids come in all languages: Reading instruction for ESL students.* Newark, DE: International Reading Association.

Stowell, C. (1994). *Step-by-step making books.* New York: Kingfisher.

Teachers' favorite books for kids. Teachers' choices 1989–1993. (1994). Newark, DE: International Reading Association.

Trelease, J. (1989). *The new read-aloud handbook* (2nd ed.). New York: Penguin.

Wells, G. (1986). *The meaning makers. Children learning language and using language to learn.* Portsmouth, NH: Heinemann.

Woods, K., & Moss, A. (1992). *Exploring literature in the classroom: Contents and methods.* Norwood, MA: Christopher-Gordon.

JOURNALS AND MAGAZINES

Book Links
American Library Association
50 E. Huron Street
Chicago, IL 60611

The Horn Book Magazine
14 Beacon St.
Boston, MA 02108

Journal of Adolescent & Adult
   Literacy
International Reading
   Association
800 Barksdale Road
P.O. Box 8139
Newark, DE 19714

Language Arts
National Council of Teachers
   of English
1111 Kenyon Road
Urbana, IL 61801

Literature Update
National Research Center on
   Literature Teaching and
   Learning
University at Albany
State University of New York
1400 Washington Avenue
Albany, NY 12222

The New Advocate
Christopher-Gordon
   Publishers
480 Washington Street
Needham Heights, MA 02062

The Reading Teacher
International Reading
   Association
800 Barksdale Road
P.O. Box 8139
Newark, DE 19714

School Library Journal
R. R. Bowker
Box 13706
Philadelphia, PA 19101

The WEB
Ohio State University
29 W. Woodruff,
200 Ramseyer Hall
Columbus, OH 43210

A P P E N D I X   B

Award-Winning Literature ⸻

THE CALDECOTT MEDAL
AND HONOR AWARDS

The Caldecott Medal, first awarded in 1938, is presented annually to the illustrator of the most distinguished picture book published in the United States. The award is named after Randolph Caldecott, a British illustrator, and is given by the Children's Services Division of the American Library Association.

1938 **Title:**   *Animals of the Bible*
       Author: Helen Dean Fish
       Illustrator: Dorothy P. Lathrop
       Publisher: Frederick A. Stokes

Honor Books: *Seven Simeons: A Russian Tale* by Boris Artzybasheff, Viking; *Four and Twenty Blackbirds: Nursery Rhymes of Yesterday Recalled for Children of Today* by Helen Dean Fish, illustrated by Robert Lawson, Frederick A. Stokes

1939 **Title:**   *Mel Li*
       Author: Thomas Handforth
       Publisher: Doubleday, Doran

Honor Books: *The Forest Pool* by Laura Adams Armer, Longmans Green; *Wee Gillis* by Munro Leaf, illustrated by Robert Lawson, Viking; *Snow White and the Seven Dwarfs* by Wanda Gag, Coward-McCann; *Barkis* by Clare Newberry, Harper and Brothers; *Andy and the Lion: A Tale of Kindness Remembered or the Power of Gratitude* by James Daugherty, Viking

117

1940 Title: *Abraham Lincoln*
       Authors: Ingri and Edgar Parin D'Aulaire
       Publisher: Doubleday Doran

Honor Books: *Cock-a-Doodle Doo: The Story of a Little Red Rooster* by Berta and Elmer Hader, Macmillan; *Madeline* by Ludwig Bemelmans, Simon & Schuster; *The Ageless Story* by Lauren Ford, Dodd Mead

1941 Title: *They Were Strong and Good*
       Author: Robert Lawson
       Publisher: Viking

Honor Book: *April's Kittens* by Clare Newberry, Harper and Brothers

1942 Title: *Make Way for Ducklings*
       Author: Robert McCloskey
       Publisher: Viking

Honor Books: *An American ABC* by Maud and Miska Petersham, Macmillan; *In My Mother's House* by Ann Nolan Clark, illustrated by Velino Herrera, Viking; *Paddle-to-the-Sea* by Holling C. Holling, Houghton Mifflin; *Nothing at All* by Wanda Gag, Coward-McCann

1943 Title: *The Little House*
       Author: Virginia Lee Burton
       Publisher: Houghton Mifflin

Honor Books: *Dash and Dart* by Mary and Conrad Buff, Viking; *Marshmallow* by Clare Newberry, Harper and Brothers

1944 Title: *Many Moons*
       Author: James Thurber
       Illustrator: Louis Slobodkin
       Publisher: Harcourt Brace

Honor Books: *Small Rain: Verses from the Bible* selected by Jessie Orton Jones, illustrated by Elizabeth Orton Jones, Viking; *Pierre Pigeon* by Lee Kingman, illustrated by Arnold E. Bare, Houghton Mifflin; *The Mighty Hunter* by Berta and

Elmer Hader, Macmillan; *A Child's Good Night Book* by Margaret Wise Brown, illustrated by Jean Charlot, W. R. Scott; *Good-Luck Horse* by Chih-Yi Chan, illustrated by Plato Chan, Whittlesey

1945 **Title:** *Prayer for a Child*
Author: Rachel Field
Illustrator: Elizabeth Orton Jones
Publisher: Macmillan

Honor Books: *Mother Goose: Seventy-Seven Verses with Pictures* illustrated by Tasha Tudor, Henry Z. Walck; *In the Forest* by Marie Hall Ets, Viking; *Yonie Wondernose* by Marguerite de Angeli, Doubleday; *The Christmas Anna Angel* by Ruth Sawyer, illustrated by Kate Seredy, Viking

1946 **Title:** *The Rooster Crows* (traditional Mother Goose)
Illustrators: Maud and Miska Petersham
Publisher: Macmillan

Honor Books: *Little Lost Lamb* by Golden MacDonald, illustrated by Leonard Weisgard, Doubleday; *Sing Mother Goose* by Opal Wheeler, illustrated by Marjorie Torrey, E. P. Dutton; *My Mother Is the Most Beautiful Woman in the World* by Becky Reyher, illustrated by Ruth Gannett, Howell, Soskin; *You Can Write Chinese* by Kurt Wiese, Viking

1947 **Title:** *The Little Island*
Author: Golden MacDonald
Illustrator: Lenord Weisgard
Publisher: Doubleday

Honor Books: *Rain Drop Splash* by Alvin Tresselt, illustrated by Leonard Weisgard, Lothrop, Lee & Shepard; *Boats on the River* by Marjorie Flack, illustrated by Jay Hyde Barnum, Viking; *Timothy Turtle* by Al Graham, illustrated by Tony Palazzo, Robert Welch; *Pedro, the Angel of Olvera Street* by Leo Politi, Charles Scribner's Sons; *Sing in Praise: A Collection of the Best-Loved Hymns* by Opal Wheeler, illustrated by Marjorie Torrey, E. P. Dutton

1948 **Title:**   *White Snow, Bright Snow*
       Author: Alvin Tresselt
       Illustrator: Roger Duvoisin
       Publisher: Lothrop, Lee & Shepard

Honor Books: *Stone Soup: An Old Tale* by Marcia Brown, Charles Scribner's Sons; *McElligot's Pool* by Dr. Seuss, Random House; *Bambino the Clown* by George Schreiber, Viking; *Roger and the Fox* by Lavinia Davis, illustrated by Hildegard Woodward, Doubleday; *Song of Robin Hood* edited by Anne Malcolmson, illustrated by Virginia Lee Burton, Houghton Mifflin

1949 **Title:**   *The Big Snow*
       Author: Betta and Elmer Hader
       Publisher: Macmillan

Honor Books: *Blueberries for Sal* by Robert McCloskey, Viking; *All around the Town* by Phyllis McGinley, illustrated by Helen Stone, J. B. Lippincott; *Juanita* by Leo Politi, Charles Scribner's Sons; *Fish in the Air* by Kurt Wiese, Viking

1950 **Title:**   *Song of the Swallows*
       Author: Leo Politi
       Publisher: Charles Scribner's Sons

Honor Books: *America's Ethan Allen* by Stewart Holbrook, illustrated by Lynd Ward, Houghton Mifflin; *The Wild Birthday Cake* by Lavinia Davis, illustrated by Hildegard Woodward, Doubleday; *The Happy Day* by Ruth Krauss, illustrated by Marc Simont, Harper and Brothers; *Bartholomew and the Oobleck* by Dr. Seuss, Random; *Henry Fisherman* by Marcia Brown, Charles Scribner's Sons

1951 **Title:**   *The Egg Tree*
       Author: Katherine Milhous
       Publisher: Charles Scribner's Sons

Honor Books: *Dick Whittington and His Cat* by Marcia Brown, Charles Scribner's Sons; *The Two Reds* by William Lipkind, illustrated by Nicholas Mordvinoff, Harcourt; *If I Ran the Zoo* by Dr. Seuss, Random House; *The Most*

Wonderful Doll in the World by Phyllis McGinley, illustrated by Helen Stone, J. B. Lippincott; *T-Bone, the Baby Sitter* by Clare Newberry, Harper and Brothers

1952 **Title:** *Finders Keepers*
Author: William Lipkind
Illustrator: Nicholas Mordvinoff
Publisher: Harcourt

Honor Books: *Mr. T. W. Anthony Wood: The Story of a Cat and a Dog and a Mouse* by Marie Hall Ets, Viking; *Skipper John's Cook* by Marcia Brown, Charles Scribner's Sons; *All Falling Down* by Gene Zion, illustrated by Margaret Bloy Graham, Harper and Brothers; *Bear Party* by William Pene du Bois, Viking; *Feather Mountain* by Elizabeth Olds, Houghton Mifflin

1953 **Title:** *The Biggest Bear*
Author: Lynd Ward
Publisher: Houghton Mifflin

Honor Books: *Puss in Boots* by Charles Perrault, illustrated and translated by Marcia Brown, Charles Scribner's Sons; *One Morning in Maine* by Robert McCloskey, Viking; *Ape in a Cape: An Alphabet of Odd Animals* by Fritz Eichenberg, Harcourt; *The Storm Book* by Charlotte Zolotow, illustrated by Margaret Bloy Graham, Harper and Brothers; *Five Little Monkeys* by Juliet Kepes, Houghton Mifflin

1954 **Title:** *Madeline's Rescue*
Author: Ludwig Bemelmans
Publisher: Viking

Honor Books: *Journey Cake, Ho!* by Ruth Sawyer, illustrated by Robert McCloskey, Viking; *When Will the World Be Mine?* by Miriam Schlein, illustrated by Jean Charlot, W. R. Scott; *The Steadfast Tin Soldier* by Hans Christian Andersen, translated by M. R. James, illustrated by Marcia Brown, Charles Scribner's Sons; *A Very Special House* by Ruth Krauss, illustrated by Maurice Sendak, Harper and Brothers; *Green Eyes* by Abe Birnbaum, Capitol

1955 Title: *Cinderella, or the Little Glass Slipper*
Author: Charles Perrault
Translator: Marcia Brown
Illustrator: Marcia Brown
Publisher: Charles Scribner's Sons

Honor Books: *Book of Nursery and Mother Goose Rhymes*, illustrated by Marguerite de Angeli, Doubleday; *Wheel on the Chimney* by Margaret Wise Brown, illustrated by Tibor Gergely, J. B. Lippincott; *The Thanksgiving Story* by Alice Dalgliesh, illustrated by Helen Sewell, Charles Scribner's Sons

1956 Title: *Frog Went A-Courtin'*
Editor: John Langstaff
Illustrator: Feodor Rojankovsky
Publisher: Harcourt

Honor Books: *Play with Me* by Marie Hall Ets, Viking; *Crow Boy* by Taro Yashima, Viking

1957 Title: *A Tree Is Nice*
Author: Janice May Udry
Illustrator: Marc Simont
Publisher: Harper and Brothers

Honor Books: *Mr. Penny's Race Horse* by Marie Hall Ets, Viking; *1 Is One* by Tasha Tudor, Henry Z. Walck; *Anatole* by Eve Titus, illustrated by Paul Galdone, Whittlesey; *Gillespie and the Guards* by Benjamin Elkin, illustrated by James Daugherty, Viking; *Lion* by William Pene du Bois, Viking

1958 Title: *Time of Wonder*
Author: Robert McCloskey
Publisher: Viking

Honor Books: *Fly High, Fly Low* by Don Freeman, Viking; *Anatole and the Cat* by Eve Titus, illustrated by Paul Galdone, Whittlesey

1959 Title: *Chanticleer and the Fox* (adapted from Chaucer)
Illustrator: Barbara Cooney
Publisher: Thomas Y. Crowell

Honor Books: *The House That Jack Built: A Picture Book in Two Languages* by Antonio Frasconi, Harcourt Brace; *What Do You Say, Dear?*, by Sesyle Joslin, illustrated by Maurice Sendak, W. R. Scott; *Umbrella* by Taro Yashima, Viking

1960 Title: *Nine Days to Christmas*
      Authors: Marie Hall Ets and Aurora Labastida
      Illustrator: Marie Hall Ets
      Publisher: Viking

Honor Books: *Houses from the Sea* by Alice E. Goudey, illustrated by Adrienne Adams, Charles Scribner's Sons; *The Moon Jumpers* by Janice May Udry, illustrated by Maurice Sendak, Harper and Brothers

1961 Title: *Baboushka and the Three Kings*
      Author: Ruth Robbins
      Illustrator: Nicolas Sidjakov
      Publisher: Parnassus Imprints

Honor Book: *Inch by Inch* by Leo Lionni, Obolensky

1962 Title: *Once a Mouse . . .*
      Author: Marcia Brown
      Publisher: Charles Scribner's Sons

Honor Books: *The Fox Went out on a Chilly Night: An Old Song* by Peter Spier, Doubleday; *Little Bear's Visit* by Else Holmelund Minarik, illustrated by Maurice Sendak, Harper and Brothers; *The Day We Saw the Sun Come Up* by Alice E. Goudey, illustrated by Adrienne Adams, Charles Scribner's Sons

1963 Title: *The Snowy Day*
      Author: Ezra Jack Keats
      Publisher: Viking

Honor Books: *The Sun Is a Golden Earring* by Natalia M. Belting, illustrated by Bernarda Bryson, Holt, Rinehart, & Winston; *Mr. Rabbit and the Lovely Present* by Charlotte Zolotow, illustrated by Maurice Sendak, Harper & Row

1964 Title: *Where the Wild Things Are*
Author: Maurice Sendak
Publisher: Harper & Row

Honor Books: *Swimmy* by Leo Lionni, Pantheon; *All in the Morning Early* by Sorche Nic Leodhas, illustrated by Evaline Ness, Holt, Rinehart, & Winston; *Mother Goose and Nursery Rhymes* illustrated by Philip Reed, Atheneum

1965 Title: *May I Bring a Friend?*
Author: Beatrice Schenk de Regniers
Illustrator: Beni Montresor
Publisher: Atheneum

Honor Books: *Rain Makes Applesauce* by Julian Scheer, illustrated by Marvin Bileck, Holiday House; *The Wave* by Margaret Hodges, illustrated by Blair Lent, Houghton Mifflin; *A Pocketful of Cricket* by Rebecca Caudill, illustrated by Evaline Ness, Holt, Rinehart, & Winston

1966 Title: *Always Room for One More*
Author: Sorche Nic Leodhas
Illustrator: Nonny Hogrogian
Publisher: Holt, Rinehart & Winston

Honor Books: *Hide and Seek Fog* by Alvin Tresselt, illustrated by Roger Duvoisin, Lothrop, Lee & Shepart; *Just Me* by Marie Hall Ets, Viking; *Tom Tit Tot* by Evaline Ness, Charles Scribner's Sons

1967 Title: *Sam, Bangs & Moonshine*
Author: Evaline Ness
Publisher: Holt, Rinehart, & Winston

Honor Book: *One Wide River to Cross* by Barbara Emberley, illustrated by Ed Emberley, Prentice-Hall

1968 Title: *Drummer Hoff*
Author: Barbara Emberley
Illustrator: Ed Emberley
Publisher: Prentice-Hall

Honor Books: *Frederick* by Leo Lionni, Pantheon; *Seashore Story* by Taro Yashima, Viking; *The Emperor and the Kite* by Jane Yolen, illustrated by Ed Young, World

1969 Title: *The Fool of the World and the Flying Ship*
Author: Arthur Ransom
Illustrator: Uri Shulevitz
Publisher: Farrar, Straus & Giroux

Honor Book: *Why the Sun and the Moon Live in the Sky: An African Folktale* by Elphinstone Dayrell, illustrated by Blair Lent, Houghton Mifflin

1970 Title: *Sylvester and the Magic Pebble*
Author: William Steig
Publisher: Windmill/Simon & Schuster

Honor Books: *Goggles!* by Ezra Jack Keats, Macmillan; *Alexander and the Wind-Up Mouse* by Leo Lionni, Pantheon; *Pop Corn and Ma Goodness* by Edna Mitchell Preston, illustrated by Robert Andrew Parker, Viking; *Thy Friend, Obadiah* by Brinton Turkle, Viking; *The Judge: An Untrue Tale* by Harve Zemach, illustrated by Margot Zemach, Farrar, Straus & Giroux

1971 Title: *A Story, A Story*
Author: Gail E. Haley
Publisher: Atheneum

Honor Books: *The Angry Moon* by William Sleator, illustrated by Blair Lent, Little, Brown; *Frog and Toad Are Friends* by Arnold Lobel, Harper & Row; *In the Night Kitchen* by Maurice Sendak, Harper & Row

1972 Title: *One Fine Day*
Author: Nonny Hogrogian
Publisher: Macmillan

Honor Books: *If All the Seas Were One Sea* by Janina Domanska, Macmillan; *Moja Means One: Swahili Counting Book* by Muriel Feelings, illustrated by Tom Feelings, Dial; *Hildilid's Night* by Cheli Duran Ryan, illustrated by Arnold Lobel, Macmillan

1973 Title: *The Funny Little Woman*
Retold by: Arlene Mosel
Illustrator: Blair Lent
Publisher: E. P. Dutton

Honor Books: *Anansi the Spider: A Tale from the Ashanti* adapted and illustrated by Gerald McDermott, Holt, Rinehart, & Winston; *Hosie's Alphabet* by Hosea, Tobias, and Lisa Baskin, illustrated by Leonard Baskin, Viking; *Snow White and the Seven Dwarfs* translated by Randall Jarrell, illustrated by Nancy Ekholm Burkert, Farrar, Straus & Giroux; *When Clay Sings* by Byrd Baylor, illustrated by Tom Bahti, Charles Scribner's Sons

1974 Title: *Duffy and the Devil*
Author: Harve Zemach
Illustrator: Margot Zemach
Publisher: Farrar, Straus & Giroux

Honor Books: *Three Jovial Huntsmen* by Susan Jeffers, Bradbury; *Cathedral: The Story of Its Construction* by David Macaulay, Houghton Mifflin

1975 Title: *Arrow to the Sun*
Adapted by: Gerald McDermott
Illustrator: Gerald McDermott
Publisher: Viking

Honor Book: *Jambo Means Hello: A Swahili Alphabet Book* by Muriel Feelings, illustrated by Tom Feelings, Dial

1976 Title: *Why Mosquitoes Buzz in People's Ears*
Retold by: Verna Aardema
Illustrators: Leo and Diane Dillon
Publisher: Dial

Honor Books: *The Desert Is Theirs* by Byrd Baylor, illustrated by Peter Parnall, Charles Scribner's Sons: *Strega Nona*, retold and illustrated by Tomie dePaola, Prentice-Hall

1977 Title: *Ashanti to Zulu: African Traditions*
Author: Margaret Musgrove

Illustrators: Leo and Diane Dillon
Publisher: Dial

Honor Books: *The Amazing Bone* by William Steig, Farrar, Straus & Giroux; *The Contest*, retold and illustrated by Nony Hogrogrian, Greenwillow; *Fish for Supper* by M. B. Goffstein, Dial; *The Golem: A Jewish Legend* by Beverly Brodsky McDermott, J. B. Lippincott; *Hawk, I'm Your Brother* by Byrd Baylor, illustrated by Peter Parnall, Charles Scribner's Sons

1978 **Title:**   *Noah's Ark*
Author: Peter Spier
Publisher: Doubleday

Honor Books: *Castle* by David Macaulay, Houghton Mifflin; *It Could Always Be Worse*, retold and illustrated by Margot Zemach, Farrar, Straus & Giroux

1979 **Title:**   *The Girl Who Loved Wild Horses*
Author: Paul Goble
Publisher: Bradbury

Honor Books: *Freight Train* by Donald Crews, Greenwillow; *The Way to Start a Day* by Byrd Baylor, illustrated by Peter Parnall, Charles Scribner's Sons

1980 **Title:**   *Ox-Cart Man*
Author: Donald Hall
Illustrator: Barbara Cooney
Publisher: Viking

Honor Books: *Ben's Trumpet* by Rachel Isadora, Greenwillow; *The Treasure* by Uri Shulevitz, Farrar, Straus & Giroux; *The Garden of Abdul Gasazi* by Chris Van Allsburg, Houghton Mifflin

1981 **Title:**   *Fables*
Author: Arnold Lobel
Publisher: Harper & Row

Honor Books: *The Bremen-Town Musicians* by Ilse Plume, Doubleday; *The Grey Lady and the Strawberry Snatcher* by

Molly Bang, Four Winds; *Mice Twice* by Joseph Low, Atheneum; Truck by Donald Crews, Greenwillow

1982 **Title:**   *Jumanji*
Author: Chris Van Allsburg
Publisher: Houghton Mifflin

Honor Books: *A Visit to William Blake's Inn: Poems for Innocent and Experienced Travelers* by Nancy Willard, illustrated by Alice and Martin Provensen, Harcourt Brace Jovanovich; *Where the Buffaloes Begin* by Olaf Baker, illustrated by Stephen Gammell, F. Warne; *On Market Street* by Arnold Lobel, illustrated by Anita Lobel, Greenwillow; *Outside over There* by Maurice Sendak, Harper & Row

1983 **Title:**   *Shadow*
Author: Blaise Cendrars
Illustrator: Marcia Brown
Publisher: Charles Scribner's Sons

Honor Books: *When I Was Young in the Mountains* by Cynthia Rylant, illustrated by Diane Goode, E. P. Dutton; *A Chair for My Mother* by Vera B. Williams, Morrow

1984 **Title:**   *The Glorious Flight: Across the Channel with Louis Bleriot, July 25, 1909*
Authors: Alice and Martin Provensen
Publisher: Viking

Honor Books: *Ten, Nine, Eight* by Molly Bang, Greenwillow; *Little Red Riding Hood*, retold and illustrated by Trina Schart Hyman, Holiday House

1985 **Title:**   *St. George and the Dragon*
Retold by: Margaret Hodges
Illustrator: Trina Schart Hyman
Publisher: Little, Brown

Honor Books: *Hansel and Gretel*, retold by Rika Lesser, illustrated by Paul O. Zelinsky, Dodd; *Have You Seen My Duckling?* by Nancy Tafuri, Greenwillow; *The Story of Jumping Mouse* by John Steptoe, Lothrop, Lee & Shepard

1986 Title: *The Polar Express*
     Author: Chris Van Allsburg
     Publisher: Houghton Mifflin

Honor Books: *King Bidgood's in the Bathtub* by Audrey Wood, illustrated by Don Wood, Harcourt Brace Jovanovich; *The Relatives Came* by Cynthia Rylant, illustrated by Stephen Gammell, Bradbury

1987 Title: *Hey, Al*
     Author: Arthur Yorinks
     Illustrator: Richard Egielski
     Publisher: Farrar, Straus & Giroux

Honor Books: *Alphabatics* by Suse MacDonald, Bradbury; *Rumpelstiltskin*, retold and illustrated by Paul O. Zelinsky, E. P. Dutton; *The Village of Round and Square Houses* by Ann Grifalconi, Little, Brown

1988 Title: *Owl Moon*
     Author: Jane Yolen
     Illustrator: John Schoenherr
     Publisher: Philomel

Honor Book: *Mufaro's Beautiful Daughters: An African Tale* by John Steptoe, Lothrop, Lee & Shepard

1989 Title: *Song and Dance Man*
     Author: Karen Ackerman
     Illustrator: Stephen Gammell
     Publisher: Alfred A. Knopf

Honor Books: *The Boy of the Three-Year Nap* by Dianne Snyder, illustrated by Allen Say, Houghton Mifflin; *Free Fall* by David Wiesner, Lothrop, Lee & Shepard; *Goldilocks*, retold and illustrated by James Marshall, Dial; *Mirandy and Brother Wind* by Patricia C. McKissack, illustrated by Jerry Pinkney, Alfred A. Knopf

1990 Title: *Lon Po Po: A Red Riding Hood Story from China*
     Author: Ed Young
     Publisher: Philomel

Honor Books: *Bill Peet: An Autobiography* by Bill Peet, Houghton Mifflin; *Color Zoo* by Lois Ehlert, J. B. Lippincott; *Hershel and the Hanukkah Goblins* by Eric Kimmel, illustrated by Trina Schart Hyman, Holiday House; *The Talking Eggs* by Robert D. San Souci, illustrated by Jerry Pinkney, Dial

1991 Title: *Black and White*
Author: Davis Macaulay
Publisher: Houghton Mifflin

Honor Books: *"More More More," Said the Baby: 3 Love Stories* by Vera B. Williams, Greenwillow; *Puss in Boots* by Charles Perrault, translated by Malcolm Arthur, illustrated by Fred Marcellino, Farrar, Straus & Giroux

1992 Title: *Tuesday*
Author: David Weisner
Publisher: Clarion

Honor Book: *Tar Beach* by Faith Ringold, Crown

1993 Title: *Mirette on the High Wire*
Author: Emily Arnold McCully
Publisher: G. P. Putnam's Sons

Honor Books: *Stinky Cheese Man and Other Fairly Stupid Tales* by Jon Scieska, illustrated by Lane Smith, Viking; *Working Cotton* by Sherley Anne Williams, illustrated by Carol Byard, Harcourt Brace; *Seven Blind Mice* by Ed Young, Philomel

1994 Title: *Grandfather's Journey*
Author: Allen Say
Publisher: Houghton Mifflin

Honor Books: *Peppe the Lamplighter* by Elisa Barton, illustrated by Ted Lewin, Lothrop, Lee & Shepard; *In the Small, Small Pond* by Denise Fleming, Henry Holt; *Owen* by Kevin Henkes, Greenwillow; *Raven: A Trickster Tale from the Pacific Northwest* by Gerald McDermott, Harcourt Brace; *Yo! Yes?* by Chris Raschka, Orchard.

1995 **Title:** *Smoky Night*
     Author: Eve Bunting
     Illustrator: David Diaz
     Publisher: Harcourt Brace

Honor Books: *John Henry* by Julius Lester, illustrated by Jerry Pickney, Dial; *Swamp Angel* by Paul Zelinsky, illustrated by Anne Issacs, E. P. Dutton; *Time Flies* by Eric Rohmann, Crown.

THE NEWBERY MEDAL AND HONOR AWARDS

The Newbery award, first presented in 1922, is given annually for the most distinguished contributions to children's literature published in the United States. The award is named after John Newbery, the first English publisher of books for children, and is given by the Children's Services Division of the American Library Association.

1922 **Title:** *The Story of Mankind*
     Author: Hendrik Willem van Loon
     Publisher: Boni & Liveright

Honor Books: *The Great Quest* by Charles Hawes, Little, Brown; *Cedric the Forester* by Bernard Marshall, Appleton; *The Old Tobacco Shop: A True Account of What Befell a Little Boy in Search of Adventure* by William Bowen, Macmillan; *The Golden Fleece and the Heroes Who Lived before Achilles* by Padriac Colum, Macmillan; *Windy Hill* by Cornelia Meigs, Macmillan

1923 **Title:** *The Voyages of Doctor Dolittle*
     Author: Hugh Lofting
     Publisher: Frederick A. Stokes

1924 **Title:** *The Dark Frigate*
     Author: Chares Hawes
     Publisher: Atlantic Monthly Press

1925 Title: *Tales from Silver Lands*
     Author: Charles Finger
     Publisher: Doubleday, Page

Honor Books: *Nicholas: A Manhattan Christmas Story* by Anne Carroll Moore, G. P. Putnams' Sons; *Dream Coach* by Anne Parrish, Macmillan

1926 Title: *Shen of the Sea*
     Author: Arthur Bowie Chrisman
     Publisher: E. P. Dutton

Honor Book: *Voyagers* by Padraic Colum, Macmillan

1927 Title: *Smoky, the Cowhorse*
     Author: Will James
     Publisher: Charles Scribner's Sons

1928 Title: *Gayneck, the Story of a Pigeon*
     Author: Dhan Gopal Mukerji
     Publisher: E. P. Dutton

Honor Books: *The Wonder Smith and His Son: A Tale from the Golden Childhood of the World* by Ella Young, Longmans, Green; *Downright Dencey* by Caroline Snedeker, Doubleday

1929 Title: *The Trumpeter of Krakow*
     Author: Eric P. Kelly
     Publisher: Macmillan

Honor Books: *Pigtail of Ah Lee Ben Loo* by John Bennett, Longmans, Green; *Millions of Cats* by Wanda Gag, Coward-McCann; *The Boy Who Was* by Grace Hallock, E. P. Dutton; *Clearing Weather* by Cornelia Meigs, Little, Brown; *Runaway Papoose* by Grace Moon, Doubleday, Doran; *Tod of the Fens* by Elinor Whitney, Macmillan

1930 Title: *Hitty, Her First Hundred Years*
     Author: Rachel Field
     Publisher: Macmillan

Honor Books: *Daughter of the Seine: The Life of Madame Roland* by Jeanette Eaton, Harper and Brothers; *Pran of*

Albania by Elizabeth Miller, Doubleday, Doran; *Jumping-Off Place* by Marian Hurd McNeely, Longmans, Green; *Tangle-Coated Horse and Other Tales: Episodes from the Fionn Saga* by Ella Young, Longmans, Green; *Vaino: A Boy of New England* by Julia Davis Adams, E. P. Dutton; *Little Blacknose* by Hildegarde Swift, Harcourt

1931 Title: *The Cat Who Went to Heaven*
Author: Elizabeth Coatsworth
Publisher: Macmillan

Honor Books: *Floating Island* by Anne Parrish, Harper and Brothers; *The Dark Star of Itza: The Story of a Pagan Princess* by Alida Malkus, Harcourt; *Queer Person* by Ralph Hubbard, Doubleday, Doran; *Mountains Are Free* by Julia Davis Adams, E. P. Dutton; *Spice and the Devil's Cave* by Agnes Hewes, Alfred A. Knopf; *Meggy Macintosh* by Elizabeth Janet Gray, Doubleday, Doran; *Garram the Hunter: The Boy of the Hill Tribes* by Herbert Best, Doubleday, Doran; *Ood-Le-Uk the Wanderer* by Alice Lide and Margaret Johansen, Little, Brown

1932 Title: *Waterless Mountain*
Author: Laura Adams Armer
Publisher: Longmans, Green

Honor Books: *The Fairy Circus* by Dorothy P. Lathrop, Macmillan; *Calico Bush* by Rachel Field, Macmillan; *Boy of the South Seas* by Eunice Tietjens, Coward-McCann; *Out of the Flame* by Eloise Lownsbery, Longmans, Green; *Jane's Island* by Marjorie Allee, Houghton Mifflin; *Truce of the Wolf and Other Tales of Old Italy* by Mary Gould Davis, Harcourt, Brace

1933 Title: *Young Fu of the Upper Yangtze*
Author: Elizabeth Foreman Lewis
Publisher: John C. Winston

Honor Books: *Swift Rivers* by Cornelia Meigs, Little, Brown; *The Railroad to Freedom: A Story of the Civil War* by Hildegarde Swift, Harcourt Brace; *Children of the Soil: A Story of Scandinavia* by Nora Burglon, Doubleday, Doran

1934 Title: *Invincible Louisa: The Story of the Author of 'Little Women'*
Author: Cornelia Meigs
Publisher: Little, Brown

Honor Books: *The Forgotten Daughter* by Caroline Snedeker, Doubleday, Doran; *Swords of Steel* by Elsie Singmaster, Houghton Mifflin; *ABC Bunny* by Wanda Gag, Coward-McCann; *Winged Girl of Knossos* by Erik Berry, Appleton-Century; *New Land* by Sarah Schmidt, R. M. McBride; *Big Tree of Bunlahy: Stories of My Own Countryside* by Padraic Colum, Macmillan; *Glory of the Seas* by Agnes Hewes, Alfred A. Knopf; *Apprentice of Florence* by Ann Kyle, Houghton Mifflin

1935 Title: *Dobry*
Author: Monica Shannon
Publisher: Viking

Honor Books: *Pageant of Chinese History* by Elizabeth Seeger, Longmans, Green; *Davy Crockett* by Constance Rourke, Harcourt Brace; *Day on Skates: The Story of a Dutch Picnic* by Hilda Van Stockum, Harper

1936 Title: *Caddie Woodlawn*
Author: Carol Ryrie Brink
Publisher: Macmillan

Honor Books: *Honk, the Moose* by Phil Stong, Dodd, Mead; *The Good Master* by Kate Seredy, Viking; *Young Walter Scott* by Elizabeth Janet Gray, Viking; *All Sail Set: A Romance of the Flying Cloud* by Armstrong Sperry, John C. Winston

1937 Title: *Roller Skates*
Author: Ruth Sawyer
Publisher: Viking

Honor Books: *Phoebe Fairchild: Her Book* by Lois Lenski, Frederick A. Stokes; *Whistler's Van* by Idwal Jones, Viking; *Golden Basket* by Ludwig Bemelmans, Viking; *Winterbound* by Margery Bianco, Viking; *Audubon* by Constance Rourke, Harcourt, Brace; *The Codfish Musket* by Agnes Hewes, Doubleday, Doran

1938 **Title:** *The White Stag*
Author: Kate Seredy
Publisher: Viking

Honor Books: *Pecos Bill* by James Cloyd Bowman, Little, Brown; *Bright Island* by Mabel Robinson, Random House; *On the Banks of Plum Creek* by Laura Ingalls Wilder, Harper and Brothers

1939 **Title:** *Thimble Summer*
Author: Elizabeth Enright
Publisher: Rinehart

Honor Books: *Nino* by Valenti Angelo, Viking; *Mr. Popper's Penguins* by Richard and Florence Atwater, Little, Brown; *"Hello the Boat!"* by Phyllis Crawford, Henry Holt; *Leader by Destiny: George Washington, Man and Patriot* by Jeanette Eaton, Harcourt Brace; *Penn* by Elizabeth Janet Gray, Viking

1940 **Title:** *Daniel Boone*
Author: James Daugherty
Publisher: Viking

Honor Books: *The Singing Tree* by Kate Seredy, Viking; *Runner of the Mountain Tops: The Life of Louis Agassiz* by Mabel Robinson, Random House; *By the Shores of Silver Lake* by Laura Ingalls Wilder, Harper and Brothers; *Boy with a Pack* by Stephen W. Meader, Harcourt, Brace

1941 **Title:** *Call It Courage*
Author: Armstrong Sperry
Publisher: Macmillan

Honor Books: *Blue Willow* by Doris Gates, Viking; *Young Mac of Fort Vancouver* by Mary Jane Carr, Thomas Y. Crowell; *The Long Winter* by Laura Ingalls Wilder, Harper and Brothers; *Nansen* by Anna Gertrude Hall, Viking

1942 **Title:** *The Matchlock Gun*
Author: Walter D. Edmonds
Publisher: Dodd, Mead

Honor Books: *Little Town on the Prairie* by Laura Ingalls Wilder, Harper and Brothers; *George Washington's World* by Genevieve Foster, Charles Scribner's Sons; *Indian Captive: The Story of Mary Jemison* by Lois Lenski, Frederick A. Stokes; *Down Ryton Water* by Eva Roe Gaggin, Viking

1943 **Title:**   *Adam of the Road*
       Author: Elizabeth Janet Gray
       Publisher: Viking

Honor Books: *The Middle Moffat* by Eleanor Estes, Harcourt, Brace; *Have You Seen Tom Thumb?* by Mabel Leigh Hunt, Frederick A. Stokes

1944 **Title:**   *Johnny Tremain*
       Author: Esther Forbes
       Publisher: Houghton Mifflin

Honor Books: *The Happy Golden Years* by Laura Ingalls Wilder, Harper and Brothers; *Fog Magic* by Julia Sauer, Viking; *Rufus M.* by Eleanor Estes, Harcourt, Brace; *Mountain Born* by Elizabeth Yates, Coward-McCann

1945 **Title:**   *Rabbit Hill*
       Author: Robert Lawson
       Publisher: Viking

Honor Books: *The Hundred Dresses* by Eleanor Estes, Harcourt, Brace; *The Silver Pencil* by Alice Dalgliesh, Charles Scribner's Sons; *Abraham Lincoln's World* by Genevieve Foster, Charles Scribner's Sons; *Lone Journey: The Life of Roger Williams* by Jeanette Eaton, Harcourt, Brace

1946 **Title:**   *Strawberry Girl*
       Author: Lois Lenski
       Publisher: J. B. Lippincott

Honor Books: *Justin Morgan Had a Horse* by Marguerite Henry, Wilcox & Follett; *The Moved-Outers* by Florence Crannell Means, Houghton Mifflin; *Bhimsa, the Dancing Bear* by Christine Weston, Charles Scribner's Sons; *New Found World* by Katherine Shippen, Viking

1947 **Title:** *Miss Hickory*
  Author: Carolyn Sherwin Bailey
  Publisher: Viking

Honor Books: *Wonderful Year* by Nancy Barnes, J. Messner; *Big Tree* by Mary and Conrad Buff, Viking; *The Heavenly Tenants* by William Maxwell, Harper and Brothers; *The Avion My Uncle Flew* by Cyrus Fisher, Appleton-Century; *The Hidden Treasure of Glaston* by Eleanore Jewett, Viking

1948 **Title:** *The Twenty-One Balloons*
  Author: William Pene du Bois
  Publisher: Viking

Honor Books: *Pancakes-Paris* by Claire Huchet Bishop, Viking; *Le Lun, Lad of Courage* by Carolyn Treffinger, Abingdon-Cokesbury; *The Quaint and Curious Quest of Johnny Longfoot* by Catherine Besterman, Bobbs Merrill; *The Cow-tail Switch, and Other West African Stories* by Harold Courlander, Henry Holt; *Misty of Chincoteague* by Marguerite Henry, Rand McNally

1949 **Title:** *King of the Wind*
  Author: Marguerite Henry
  Publisher: Rand McNally

Honor Books: *Seabird* by Holling C. Holling, Houghton Mifflin; *Daughter of the Mountains* by Louis Rankin, Viking; *My Father's Dragon* by Ruth S. Gannett, Random House; *Story of the Negro* by Arna Bontemps, Alfred A. Knopf

1950 **Title:** *The Door in the Wall*
  Author: Marguerite de Angeli
  Publisher: Doubleday

Honor Books: *Tree of Freedom* by Rebecca Caudill, Viking; *The Blue Cat of Castle Town* by Catherine Coblentz, Longmans, Green; *Kildee House* by Rutherford Montgomery, Doubleday; *George Washington* by Genevieve Foster, Charles Scribner's Sons; *Song of the Pines: A Story of Norwegian Lumbering in Wisconsin* by Walter and Marion Havighurst, John C. Winston

1951 **Title:**   *Amos Fortune, Free Man*
        Author: Elizabeth Yates
        Publisher: E. P. Dutton

Honor Books: *Better Known as Johnny Appleseed* by Mabel Leigh Hunt, J. B. Lippincott; *Gandhi, Fighter without a Sword* by Jeanette Eaton, Morrow; *Abraham Lincoln, Friend of the People* by Clara Ingram Judson, Wilcox & Follett; *The Story of Appleby Capple* by Anne Parrish, Harper

1952 **Title:**   *Ginger Pye*
        Author: Eleanor Estes
        Publisher: Harcourt, Brace

Honor Books: *Americans before Columbus* by Elizabeth Baity, Viking; *Minn of the Mississippi* by Holling C. Holling, Houghton Mifflin; *The Defender* by Nicholas Kalashnikoff, Charles Scribner's Sons; *The Light at Tern Rock* by Julia Sauer, Viking; *The Apple and the Arrow* by Mary and Conrad Buff, Houghton Mifflin

1953 **Title:**   *Secret of the Andes*
        Author: Ann Nolan Clark
        Publisher: Viking

Honor Books: *Charlotte's Web* by E. B. White, Harper; *Moccasin Trail* by Eloise McGraw, Coward-McCann; *Red Sails to Capri* by Ann Weil, Viking; *The Bears on Hemlock Mountain* by Alice Dalgliesh, Charles Scribner's Sons; *Birthdays of Freedom*, Vol. 1, by Genevieve Foster, Charles Scribner's Sons

1954 **Title:**   *. . . and now Miguel*
        Author: Joseph Krumgold
        Publisher: Thomas Y. Crowell

Honor Books: *All Alone* by Claire Huchet Bishop, Viking; *Shadrach* by Meindert DeJong, Harper; *Hurry Home, Candy* by Meindert DeJong, Harper; *Theodore Roosevelt, Fighting Patriot* by Clara Ingram Judson, Follett; *Magic Maize* by Mary and Conrad Buff, Houghton Mifflin

1955 **Title:** *The Wheel on the School*
Author: Meindert DeJong
Publisher: Harper

Honor Books: *The Courage of Sarah Noble* by Alice Dalgliesh, Charles Scribner's Sons; *Banner in the Sky* by James Ullman, J. B. Lippincott

1956 **Title:** *Carry on, Mr. Bowditch*
Author: Jean Lee Latham
Publisher: Houghton Mifflin

Honor Books: *The Secret River* by Marjorie Kinnan Rawlings, Charles Scribner's Sons; *The Golden Name Day* by Jennie Lindquist, Harper; *Men, Microscopes, and Living Things* by Katherine Shippen, Viking

1957 **Title:** *Miracles on Maple Hill*
Author: Virginia Sorensen
Publisher: Harcourt Brace

Honor Books: *Old Yeller* by Fred Gipson, Harper; *The House of Sixty Fathers* by Meindert DeJong, Harper; *Mr. Justice Holmes* by Clara Ingram Judson, Follett; *The Corn Grows Ripe* by Dorothy Rhoads, Viking; *Black Fox of Lorne* by Marguerite de Angeli, Doubleday

1958 **Title:** *Rifles for Watie*
Author: Harold Keith
Publisher: Thomas Y. Crowell

Honor Books: *The Horsecatcher* by Mari Sandoz, Westminister; *Gone-Away Lake* by Elizabeth Enright, Harcourt, Brace; *The Great Wheel* by Robert Lawson, Viking; *Tom Paine, Freedom's Apostle* by Leo Gurko, Thomas Y. Crowell

1959 **Title:** *The Witch of Blackbird Pond*
Author: Elizabeth George Speare
Publisher: Houghton Mifflin

Honor Books: *The Family Under the Bridge* by Natalie Savage Carlson, Harper; *Along Came a Dog* by Meindert

DeJong, Harper; *Chucaro: Wild Pony of the Pampa* by Francis Kalnay, Harcourt, Brace; *The Perilous Road* by William O. Steele, Harcourt, Brace

1960 **Title:**   *Onion John*
       Author: Joseph Krumgold
       Publisher: Thomas Y. Crowell

Honor Books: *My Side of the Mountain* by Jean George, E. P. Dutton; *America is Born* by Gerald W. Johnson, Morrow; *The Gammage Cup* by Carol Kendall, Harcourt, Brace

1961 **Title:**   *Island of the Blue Dolphins*
       Author: Scott O'Dell
       Publisher: Houghton Mifflin

Honor Books: *America Moves Forward* by Gerald W. Johnson, Morrow; *Old Ramon* by Jack Schaefer, Houghton Mifflin; *The Cricket in Times Square* by George Selden, Farrar, Straus

1962 **Title:**   *The Bronze Bow*
       Author: Elizabeth George Speare
       Publisher: Houghton Mifflin

Honor Books: *Frontier Living* by Edwin Tunis, World; *The Golden Goblet* by Eloise McCraw, Coward-McCann; *Belling the Tiger* by Mary Stolz, Harper

1963 **Title:**   *A Wrinkle in Time*
       Author: Madeleine L'Engle
       Publisher: Farrar, Straus

Honor Books: *Thistle and Thyme: Tales and Legends from Scotland* by Sorche Nic Leodhas, Holt, Rinehart, & Winston; *Men of Athens* by Olivia Coolidge, Houghton Mifflin

1964 **Title:**   *It's Like This, Cat*
       Author: Emily Cheney Neville
       Publisher: Harper & Row

Honor Books: *Rascal* by Sterling North, E. P. Dutton; *The Loner* by Ester Wier, D. McKay

1965 Title: *Shadow of a Bull*
Author: Maia Wojciechowska
Publisher: Antheneum

Honor Book: *Across Five Aprils* by Irene Hunt, Follett

1966 Title: *I, Juan de Pareja*
Author: Elizabeth Borten de Trevino
Publisher: Farrar, Straus & Giroux

Honor Books: *The Black Cauldron* by Lloyd Alexander, Holt, Rinehart, & Winston; *The Animal Family* by Randall Jarrell, Pantheon; *The Noonday Friends* by Mary Stolz, Harper & Row

1967 Title: *Up a Road Slowly*
Author: Irene Hunt
Publisher: Follett

Honor Books: *The King's Fifth* by Scott O'Dell, Houghton Mifflin; *Zlateh the Goat and Other Stories* by Isaac Bashevis Singer, Harper & Row; *The Jazz Man* by Mary H. Weik, Atheneum

1968 Title: *From the Mixed-Up Files of Mrs. Basil E. Frankweiler*
Author: E. L. Konigsburg
Publisher: Atheneum

Honor Books: *Jennifer, Hecate, Macbeth, William McKinley, and Me, Elizabeth* by E. L. Konigsburg, Atheneum; *The Black Pearl* by Scott O'Dell, Houghton Mifflin; *The Fearsome Inn* by Isaac Bashevis Singer, Charles Scribner's Sons; *The Egypt Game* by Zilpha Keatley Synder, Atheneum

1969 Title: *The High King*
Author: Lloyd Alexander
Publisher: Holt, Rinehart, & Winston

Honor Books: *To Be a Slave* by Julius Lester, Dial; *When Shlemiel Went to Warsaw and Other Stories* by Isaac Bashevis Singer, Farrar, Straus & Giroux

1970 Title: *Sounder*
Author: William H. Armstrong
Publisher: Harper & Row

Honor Books: *Our Eddie* by Sulamith Ish-Kishor, Pantheon; *The Many Ways of Seeing: An Introduction to the Pleasures of Art* by Janet Gaylord Moore, World; *Journey Outside* by Mary Q. Steele, Viking

1971 Title: *Summer of the Swans*
Author: Betsy Byars
Publisher: Viking

Honor Books: *Kneeknock Rise* by Natalie Babbitt, Farrar, Straus & Giroux; *Enchantress from the Stars* by Sylvia Louise Engdahl, Atheneum; *Sing Down the Moon* by Scott O'Dell, Houghton Mifflin

1972 Title: *Mrs. Frisby and the Rats of NIMH*
Author: Robert C. O'Brien
Publisher: Atheneum

Honor Books: *Incident at Hawk's Hill* by Allan W. Eckert, Little, Brown; *The Planet of Junior Brown* by Virginia Hamilton, Macmillan; *The Tombs of Atuan* by Ursula K. Le Guin, Atheneum; *Annie and the Old One* by Miska Miles, Little, Brown; *The Headless Cupid* by Zilpha Keatley Snyder, Atheneum

1973 Title: *Julie of the Wolves*
Author: Jean Craighead George
Publisher: Harper & Row

Honor Books: *Frog and Toad Together* by Arnold Lobel, Harper & Row; *The Upstairs Room* by Johanna Reiss, Thomas Y. Crowell; *The Witches of Worm* by Zilpha Keatley Snyder, Atheneum

1974 **Title:**　　*The Slave Dancer*
　　　　Author:　　Paula Fox
　　　　Publisher:　Bradbury

　　Honor Book: *The Dark is Rising* by Susan Cooper, Atheneum

1975 **Title:**　　*M. C. Higgins, the Great*
　　　　Author:　　Virginia Hamilton
　　　　Publisher:　Macmillan

　　Honor Books: *Figgs & Phantoms* by Ellen Raskin, E. P. Dutton; *My Brother Sam is Dead* by James Lincoln Collier and Christopher Collier, Four Winds; *The Perilous Gard* by Elizabeth Marie Pope, Houghton Mifflin; *Philip Hall Likes Me, I Reckon Maybe* by Bette Greene, Dial

1976 **Title:**　　*The Grey King*
　　　　Author:　　Susan Cooper
　　　　Publisher:　Atheneum

　　Honor Books: *The Hundred Penny Box* by Sharon Bell Mathis, Viking; *Dragonwings* by Laurence Yep, Harper & Row

1977 **Title:**　　*Roll of Thunder, Hear My Cry*
　　　　Author:　　Mildred D. Taylor
　　　　Publisher:　Dial

　　Honor Books: *Abel's Island* by William Steig, Farrar, Straus & Giroux; *A String in the Harp* by Nancy Bond, Atheneum

1978 **Title:**　　*Bridge to Terabithia*
　　　　Author:　　Katherine Paterson
　　　　Publisher:　Thomas Y. Crowell

　　Honor Books: *Ramona and Her Father* by Beverly Cleary, Morrow; *Anpao: An American Indian Odyssey* by Jamake Highwater, J. B. Lippincott

1979 **Title:**　　*The Westing Game*
　　　　Author:　　Ellen Raskin
　　　　Publisher:　E. P. Dutton

　　Honor Book: *The Great Gilly Hopkins* by Katherine Paterson, Thomas Y. Crowell

1980 Title: *A Gathering of Days: A New England Girl's Journal 1830–32*
Author: Joan Blos
Publisher: Charles Scribner's Sons

Honor Book: *The Road from Home: The Story of an Armenian Girl* by David Kherdian, Morrow

1981 Title: *Jacob Have I Loved*
Author: Katherine Paterson
Publisher: Thomas Y. Crowell

Honor Books: *The Fledgling* by Jane Langton, Harper & Row; *A Ring of Endless Light* by Madeleine L'Engle, Farrar, Straus & Giroux

1982 Title: *A Visit to William Blake's Inn: Poems for Innocent and Experienced Travelers*
Author: Nancy Willard
Publisher: Harcourt Brace Jovanovich

Honor Books: *Ramona Quimby, Age 8* by Beverly Cleary, Morrow; *Upon the Head of the Goat: A Childhood in Hungary, 1939–1944* by Aranka Siegal, Farrar, Straus & Giroux

1983 Title: *Dicey's Song*
Author: Cynthia Voigt
Publisher: Atheneum

Honor Books: *Blue Sword* by Robin McKinley, Greenwillow; *Doctor DeSoto* by William Steig, Farrar, Straus & Giroux; *Graven Images* by Paul Fleischman, Harper & Row; *Homesick: My Own Story* by Jean Fritz, Putnam; *Sweet Whisper, Brother Rush* by Virginia Hamilton, Philomel

1984 Title: *Dear Mr. Henshaw*
Author: Beverly Cleary
Publisher: Morrow

Honor Books: *The Sign of the Beaver* by Elizabeth George Speare, Houghton Mifflin; *A Solitary Blue* by Cynthia Voigt, Atheneum; *The Wish Giver* by Bill Brittain, Harper & Row; *Sugaring Time* by Kathryn Lasky, Macmillan

1985 Title: *The Hero and the Crown*
         Author: Robin McKinley
         Publisher: Greenwillow

         Honor Books: *Like Jake and Me* by Mavis Jukes, Alfred A. Knopf; *The Moves Make the Man* by Bruce Brooks, Harper & Row; *One-Eyed Cat* by Paula Fox, Bradbury

1986 Title: *Sarah, Plain and Tall*
         Author: Patricia MacLachlan
         Publisher: Harper & Row

         Honor Books: *Commodore Perry in the Land of the Shogun* by Rhoda Blumberg, Lothrop, Lee & Shepard; *Dogsong* by Gary Paulsen, Bradbury

1987 Title: *The Whipping Boy*
         Author: Sid Fleischman
         Publisher: Greenwillow

         Honor Books: *A Fine White Dust* by Cynthia Rylant, Bradbury; *On My Honor* by Marion Dane Bauer, Clarion; *Volcano: The Eruption and Healing of Mount St. Helens* by Patricia Lauber, Bradbury

1988 Title: *Lincoln: A Photobiography*
         Author: Russell Freedman
         Publisher: Clarion

         Honor Books: *After the Rain* by Norma Fox Mazer, Morrow; *Hatchet* by Gary Paulsen, Bradbury

1989 Title: *Joyful Noise: Poems for Two Voices*
         Author: Paul Fleischman
         Publisher: Harper & Row

         Honor Books: *In the Beginning: Creation Stories from Around the World* by Virginia Hamilton, Harcourt Brace Jovanovich; *Scorpions* by Walter Dean Myers, Harper & Row

1990 Title: *Number the Stars*
         Author: Lois Lowry
         Publisher: Houghton Mifflin

Honor Books: *Afternoon of the Elves* by Janet Taylor Lisle, Orchard; *Shabanu, Daughter of the Wind* by Susan Fisher Staples, Alfred A. Knopf; *The Winter Room* by Gary Paulsen, Orchard

1991 Title: *Maniac Magee*
Author: Jerry Spinelli
Publisher: Little, Brown

Honor Book: *The True Confessions of Charlotte Doyle* by Avi, Orchard

1992 Title: *Shiloh*
Author: Phyllis Reynolds Naylor
Publisher: Atheneum

Honor Books: *Nothing but the Truth* by Avi, Orchard; *Wright Brothers* by Russell Freedman, Holiday House

1993 Title: *Missing May*
Author: Cynthia Rylant
Publisher: Orchard

Honor Books: *What Hearts* by Bruce Brooks, HarperCollins; *Dark Thirty: Southern Tales of the Supernatural* by Patricia C. McKissack, Alfred A. Knopf; *Somewhere in the Darkness* by Walter Dean Myers, Scholastic

1994 Title: *The Giver*
Author: Lois Lowry
Publisher: Houghton Mifflin

Honor Books: *Crazy Lady!* by Jane Leslie Conly, HarperCollins; *Dragon's Gate* by Laurence Yep, HarperCollins; *Eleanor Roosevelt: A Life of Discovery* by Russell Freedman, Clarion

1995 Title: *Walk Two Moons*
Author: Sharon Creech
Publisher: HarperCollins

Honor Books: *Catherine, Called Birdy* by Karen Cushman, Clarion; *The Ear, the Eye, and the Arm* by Nancy Farmer, Orchard

Index